# Counselling
# for Depression

In Appreciation of your help and
guidance over the years.
Best wishes
Paul.

# Counselling in Practice

Series editor: Windy Dryden
Associate editor: E. Thomas Dowd

*Counselling in Practice* is a series of books developed especially for counsellors and students of counselling which provides practical, accessible guidelines for dealing with clients with specific, but very common, problems.

# Counselling for Depression

Paul Gilbert

SAGE Publications
London • Newbury Park • New Delhi

First published 1992

 SAGE Publications Ltd
6 Bonhill Street
London EC2A 4PU

SAGE Publications Inc
2455 Teller Road
Newbury Park, California 91320

SAGE Publications India Pvt Ltd
32, M-Block Market
Greater Kailash – I
New Delhi 110 048

**British Library Cataloguing in Publication Data**

Gilbert, Paul
  Counselling for Depression. –
  (Counselling in Practice Series)
  I. Title II. Series
  362.2

  ISBN 0–8039–8497–9
  ISBN 0–8039–8498–7 (pbk)

**Library of Congress catalog card number 92–050481**

Typeset by Mayhew Typesetting, Rhayader, Powys
Printed in Great Britain by Billing and Sons Ltd, Worcester

# Contents

# Preface

Cognitive therapy began in America some thirty years ago. Since that time, it has seen enormous developments in the client groups treated and in its therapeutic approach. Two areas that have seen important changes to the early formulations are a renewed focus on the therapeutic relationship (e.g. Beck et al., 1990; Safran and Segal, 1990) and an increased focus on interpersonal cognitive processes (e.g. Bowlby, 1980; Liotti, 1988; Safran and Segal, 1990). Both these concerns are a main focus in this book. In 1988 Trower et al. published *Cognitive-behavioural Counselling in Action*. They outlined the basic techniques and issues of the cognitive approach. The present volume, for the Counselling in Practice series, is designed to build on their introduction. It explores interpersonal counselling with a particular client group – depressed people.

The aims of this book are to focus on the interpersonal themes in counselling depressed clients, including those of the therapeutic relationship. The book is divided into two sections of four chapters each. Chapter 1 addresses issues of the nature of depression and the therapeutic relationship. Here I try to capture something of the nature of the depressive experience and focus on important counsellor skills. Chapter 2 explores the central issues of interpersonal approaches, the basic domains of relationships and how these are affected in depression. Chapter 3 outlines the basic premises of the cognitive approach and why cognitive counsellors are particularly concerned with the construction of internal meaning, ways of attributing causes to things, and basic attitudes and beliefs. Chapter 4 explores the many ways of conceptualizing therapeutic intervention and challenging dysfunctional thoughts and attitudes.

The second section aims to build on these concepts, and lead the reader through a step-by-step approach to the process of counselling the depressed person. Counselling scenarios are given to illuminate specific points and highlight types of intervention. Most of these scenarios are not derived directly from taped interviews (although some are) but from notes made at the end of sessions. They are not meant to represent exact scenes but rather to indicate and highlight issues. All client names have been changed, and minor alterations introduced in the history, to avoid identification. Chapter 5 outlines the issues that arise during the early parts of the therapy, and how to engage and agree shared understandings and goals of counselling. Chapter 6 explores the kinds of issues that arise in the middle of counselling, as the counsellor and client engage in deeper explorations and seek opportunities for change. Chapter 7 looks at some special problems that arise in depressed clients. Special attention is given to shame, guilt, envy and idealizing which often figure prominently in depressive experience. Chapter 8 explores termination issues and offers some personal reflections.

# Acknowledgements

Special thanks go to the series editor, Professor W. Dryden, for asking me to attempt this endeavour, and his encouragement during the writing. His advice was, as always, invaluable. He worked hard on the manuscript, and tried to steer me away from obscurity and lapsing into evolutionary theory. Appreciation goes to Dr C. Gillespie for his support and advice, and his comments on various chapters. Many thanks also go to Susan Worsey and Sue Ashton, who both worked hard on the text. I am indebted to the many clients who, over the years, have shared their depressive experience with me and enabled me to learn from them. They have been the best teachers. Gratitude also goes to Nell Hadlow who helped to correct the manuscript and get it into readable form. Thanks also to Joyce Chantrill and Pat Gibbins.

To Jean, Hannah and James,
who love and support me,
the many clients who have guided
and taught me, and
Professor A.T. Beck who got us all
thinking cognitively and revolutionized the
psychological treatment of depression

# PART I: DEPRESSION AND THE BASIC PRINCIPLES OF COGNITIVE-INTERPERSONAL COUNSELLING

## 1

## Depression and Dysphoria and the Counselling Relationship

Depression haunts the lives of many. It exists in many forms, takes various guises and has been recognized for many centuries. Over two thousand years ago the Greek physician Hippocrates labelled it melancholia. The Greeks believed depression arose from a disturbance of the body humours, specifically black bile. Early reports of depression can be found in numerous biblical texts. King Solomon is believed to have suffered from an evil spirit and dark moods from which he eventually killed himself. The book of Job is regarded as the work of a depressive. More recent sufferers include composers (Gustave Mahler, Tchaikovsky, Sibelius), politicians (Abraham Lincoln and Winston Churchill) and numerous writers, artists and poets (Edgar Allen Poe and Thomas Mann). Whatever else we may say about depression, it seems that it has been with us for a very long time. Indeed, it is not even unique to humans, and various animal models of depression have been advanced and researched.

### What is depression?

Depression affects us in many different ways and symptoms are spread over different aspects of functioning:

Motivation: Apathy, loss of energy and interest: things seem pointless, hopeless.

Emotional: Depressed mood, plus emptiness, anger or resentment, anxiety, shame, guilt.

Cognitive: Poor concentration, negative ideas about the self, the world and the future.

Biological: Sleep disturbance, loss of appetite, changes in hormones and brain chemicals.

Depression can vary in terms of the relative degree and severity of these symptoms, their duration and their frequency. Hence individuals can vary as to whether their depression is mild, moderate or severe, and they may have one episode or many episodes. Depression is often a major factor in various other conditions such as social anxiety, eating disorders, substance abuse, schizophrenia, and so forth. Depression can be triggered by life events (for example, depression may follow childbirth or the loss of a relationship) and life events may also be involved in recovery (for example, beginning a new relationship; Brown, 1989). Depression can have an acute onset (within days or weeks) or come on gradually (over months or years). Depression can be chronic (for example, lasting over two years), or short-lived (recovery coming in weeks or months). Some depressions also show cyclical patterns.

Paykel (1989) outlines the current proposed ICD-10 classification of depression which is being developed by the World Health Organisation. This system distinguishes a number of different types of depression:

1 Bipolar Affective Disorder: current episode of manic, hypomanic, depressed or mixed.
2 Depressive Episode: mild, (a) without somatic symptoms; (b) with somatic symptoms. Moderate, (a) without somatic symptoms; (b) with somatic symptoms. Severe, (a) without psychotic symptoms; (b) with psychotic symptoms. Psychotic symptoms may be further divided into mood congruent (e.g. delusions of poverty or guilt) and mood incongruent delusions (e.g. paranoid).
3 Recurrent Depressive Disorder: current episode of depressive disorder.
4 Persistent Affective Disorder: (a) cyclothymia; (b) dysthymia.
5 Other Mood (Affective) Disorders: specified/unspecified.

Paykel (1989) points out that as about 50 per cent of depressives will have subsequent episodes there is little point in separating out recurrent depression (3) as a separate type.

There is increasing evidence for a form of depression called Seasonal Affective Disorder. This condition has some atypical symptoms, including a seasonal onset (autumn and winter) with relief in the spring and summer. Mood change is associated with increased appetite, especially for carbohydrates, weight gain and increased sleep. This is an important distinction since exposure to bright light has been shown to be a promising, effective and quick treatment for this condition (Kasper and Rosenthal, 1989).

*How common is depression?*
To answer this question, much depends on the definition of depression and the precision of the diagnosis. If we use modern methods of classifying depression, then the figures suggest that one person per thousand will be hospitalized for a depressive disorder, and another two per thousand will be referred to psychiatrists (Paykel, 1989). However, varying numbers (3–10 per cent) may seek treatment from other sources such as general practitioners, social workers and counsellors. If we loosen the criteria, then rates of depression rise remarkably. We also know that many who are depressed do not seek treatment, and of those who do, their treatment is often inadequate.

In general, some estimates suggest that as many as one person in four or five will have an episode of serious depression warranting treatment at some point in their lives, although this may be a very conservative figure depending on social class and other social demographic variables (Bebbington et al., 1989). Worldwide, a figure of 100 million depressives has been estimated. What is most worrying is that depression may be on the increase (Klerman, 1988). There are many reasons for this, including demographic changes, life-style changes, increased use of drugs with depressive side effects, and social stresses of various forms (Gilbert, 1992). A counsellor who makes depression a special source of study will have no shortage of cases.

*The course of depression*
Some clients will recover very quickly and most clients will show some recovery in the first six months, but as many as 20 per cent of cases may have a chronic course; that is, the person can remain depressed at varying levels of severity for two years or more (Scott, 1988). Some clients suffer acute episodes that are superimposed on milder chronic conditions. About 50 per cent of clients with diagnosed depression will relapse (Belsher and Costello, 1988) regardless of treatment, although cognitive counselling shows some promise in being able to reduce this rate. Criticism from spouse is one of the more powerful predictors of relapse (Hooley and Teasdale, 1989).

*The assessment of depression*
There are many ways of assessing depression and as we have seen depression can be subdivided into various types. Generally, a counsellor rarely makes a detailed diagnosis of type, and some counsellors even wonder about the wisdom of distinguishing depression from other psychological difficulties. Assessment will

often focus on the following key areas:

*Psychological*

1 What does the client think and feel about him/herself? Especially important is attributional style (a tendency to self-blame) and social comparison (feelings of being less able, less competent than others or different in some way).
2 What does the client think and feel about the future?
3 What are the client's current life circumstances?
4 How long has the client felt depressed?
5 Is the depression a change from his/her normal mood state or an accentuation of more chronic low mood? Is there loss of enjoyment of previously enjoyed activities (e.g. sex, meeting friends, going out)?
6 Does the client see his/her depression in psychological and/or relationship terms, or is there a belief that he or she is physically ill? (Strong beliefs in physical illness can make short-term counselling difficult.)

*Social*

1 Are there any major life events or upsets that might have triggered the depression?
2 What are the client's perceptions of social relationships? Have there been major losses? Is the home environment aggressive or neglectful? Does the client have feelings of hostility to others and/or feelings of being let down?
3 What are the sources of social support, friends and family relationships? Can the client use these if available or have they gradually withdrawn from social contact?
4 Does an unstimulating social environment (e.g. boredom) play a role? Boredom is a more common problem in depression than is currently recognized.
5 Are there major practical problems that may need other sources of help? (e.g. social work for accommodation problems or advice for financial problems). Practical problems can sometimes be overlooked.

*Biological*

1 Is there sleep disturbance (early morning waking, waking after being asleep for a short period and/or difficulties getting to sleep)?
2 Are there major changes in appetite and weight?
3 How serious is fatigue and loss of energy?
4 Psychomotor changes, especially agitation and retardation, should be noted. If a client is very slowed up and finds it

difficult to concentrate this can hamper counselling. Severe retardation and lowered concentration may be a poor prognostic indicator for short-term counselling.

5 Would a trial of antidepressant drugs help to break up a depressive pattern? Most studies suggest that antidepressants do not interfere with counselling and are certainly indicated if the depression is severe.

The most commonly used, and well-researched, self-report scale for depression is the Beck Depression Inventory (Beck et al., 1979). This scale not only allows the counsellor to gain an overall impression of the patterns of symptoms, but also can be used to monitor recovery. A general overview of measuring instruments for depression can be found in Ferguson and Tyrer (1989), Gotlib and Cane (1989), Berndt (1990) and Sholomskas (1990).

The counsellor is also interested in the other affects (or emotions) of depression. In some cases it can be anxiety. Various anxiety conditions often get worse when a client is depressed. In some of these cases helping the anxiety lifts the depression. For other cases it is the reverse. Other affects may include strong hostility or passive, unexpressed aggression (this is often noted from the nonverbal behaviour of the client), envy, guilt or shame.

In general, a counsellor should be able to assess the main areas of functioning noted above. The other area to be familiar with is the risk of suicide in depressed clients (Hawton, 1987). The Beck Depression Inventory allows for this and indicates a potential danger requiring further exploration. Depending on their expertise, counsellors may wish to gain outside advice. A combination of a desire to harm self and hopelessness are warning signs. For treatment of suicidal clients see Hawton (1987), Hawton and Catalan (1987), Grollman (1988) and Williams and Wells (1989).

*Treating depression*

There have been many different treatments suggested for depression, including drugs and ECT, and a plethora of psychosocial interventions. These include psychoanalysis, family therapy, behaviour therapy and social skills training, affect therapy, interpersonal therapy and cognitive therapy. This book will take the cognitive-interpersonal approach; that is, our concern will be with the internal cognitive processes of depression, with a special focus on interpersonal cognitions, social roles and behaviour. For a discussion of family or marital counselling, see Gotlib and Colby (1987), Clarkin et al. (1988) and Beach et al. (1990).

Poor prognostic indicators for the approach outlined here

include: severe depression, making it difficult for the client to form a therapeutic contract; a clear belief that the client is suffering from a physical illness; chronicity; and clear evidence of cyclical depression. These kinds of difficulties may require alternative interventions or at least other interventions to run in tandem with the psychological approach.

The counsellor should also be aware that all depressed states have biological effects and some are related to hormonal/biological changes (e.g. thyroid, the menopause, head injury etc.). There is recent concern that some depressions have become over 'psychologicalized', missing important physical causes (Goudsmit and Gadd, 1991). On the other hand, poverty, poor social conditions, lack of social support and negative life events also increase the risk of depression, while positive life events are associated with recovery (Brown, 1989). Consequently, the approach here endorses the biopsychosocial model of depression (Vasile et al., 1987; Gilbert, 1992). This model is concerned with different levels of functioning rather than simple models of causality.

Although there are clients for whom this approach may not be suited, there are many, perhaps the majority, for whom it will be (see Hollon et al., 1991, for a recent review of the evidence on the efficacy of cognitive therapy for depression). The following chapters outline some of the central issues of working with depressed clients, discuss the various skills and qualities that are necessary for the counsellor and how these can be embedded in the cognitive-interpersonal approach. Because the focus is on internal meaning and interpersonal behaviour, this approach places greater emphasis on the therapeutic relationship than is common in cognitive counselling. For this reason, the rest of this chapter will focus on the therapeutic relationship since, without a good grasp of this, counsellors can themselves be a source of resistance to change. Some key concepts that will be helpful in working with depressed people are outlined below.

## The helping relationship

There are a large number of models of helping, many of which are excellently reviewed by Corey (1991). Although counsellors differ in their focus and how they work, there are some central aspects that most share. First is the recognition that the counselling relationship is a special kind of relationship in which the client needs to be understood – not only in a superficial sense by what they say, but also in a deeper sense, that is to make contact with their internal experiences. Dryden (1989b) provides an excellent introduction to these issues: understanding the basic structures of counselling, the process and stages of counselling, issues of transference and counter-transference, dealing with reluctant and resistant clients and termination issues.

Here we focus on selective aspects of the therapeutic relationship that are of special interest to those working with depressed clients. Two counsellors can be noted – Carl Rogers and Heinz Kohut. There are, in fact, many overlaps between them, as noted by Kahn (1985, 1989), and they were at the same university (Chicago) for ten years, although they do not seem to have acknowledged each other.

## Carl Rogers (1902–87)

Rogers (1957) was one of the first counsellors to emphasize the relationship between counsellor and client as a source of healing. He argued that the therapeutic relationship should have three basic elements: (a) accurate empathy; (b) congruence, genuineness and 'counsellor realness'; and (c) unconditional positive regard.

Much has been written on the nature of accurate empathy and what this entails (Goldstein and Michaels, 1985) and we shall return to this below. 'Counsellor realness' means that the counsellor should act in a genuine way and not mask feelings or pretend. However, others think that there are limits to the non-masking of feelings in counselling and doubt the value of expressing negative feelings to clients (Kahn, 1985), especially with depressed clients. In general, there should not be 'a counselling persona' that one puts on when one sees the client. Nor should the counsellor slip into a detached and technique-orientated mode of relating. The client's awareness that the person of the counsellor is 'with them' in the session provides an important interpersonal experience. This is particularly important for depressed people because they often feel separate and cut off from others and think that others cannot be bothered with them or understand them.

The therapeutic atmosphere should be one of warmth and engagement, rather than one of technique-focused detachment. The counsellor should provide an atmosphere of genuine care and concern rather than a 'job-orientated role'. These experiences in Rogers' view were both necessary and sufficient to enable the client to find within themselves the solutions to their own problems.

## Heinz Kohut (1913–81)

Kohut (1977) went further than Rogers, and argued that there were certain kinds of internal experience that the client needed to be understood and recognized. These were (a) the need to feel valued and approved of (*mirroring*); (b) the need to have others whom he/she can turn to and feel comforted by (*idealizing*); and (c) the need to feel like others (*belonging*).

*Mirroring:* The need to be valued and approved of arises from a child's early exhibitionist behaviour (the 'look at me, daddy, watch me do this' behaviour). When a parent mirrors pride to the child ('well done, that's very good') the child internalizes a good and vigorous sense of self. For example, if a child shows off and the parent praises the child, then the child experiences him/herself as able and good. Thus the internal experience to 'showing off' cues a positive affect. If, however, the parent repeatedly puts the child down ('don't do that, you look stupid'), or shows no interest, then the child experiences him/herself as bad, shameful or ineffective to influence the attentions of others. Thus Kohut argued that social interactions give rise to 'self objects'. A self object is an internal experience of the self (not just a memory of how others have responded). Our self object relationships (internal experiences) are usually elicited in social roles (see Gilbert, 1992). For example, in social situations I might experience myself as incompetent and feel shame/embarrassment. This shame/embarrassment reflects a self object experience 'me as ashamed'.

Morrison (1984) notes Kohut's distinction of 'defensive self-structures' which mobilize efforts to conceal deficits in self, and 'compensatory self-structures' which mobilize efforts to make up for a weakness in self, literally to compensate. Morrison offers a complex but interesting idea that depression often results from the inability to maintain compensatory structures. The individual simply cannot achieve the ideals which are necessary (be it via a relationship or personal effort) to lift self-esteem and restore a sense of self-cohesion and vigour. He notes similarities with Bibring's (1953) concepts, but unlike Bibring he places shame as a central affect. Understanding shame helps us to understand narcissistic rage, especially in depression (Mollon and Parry, 1984) as we shall note in chapter 7.

In counselling, clients need to have recognized and understood their needs to be approved of, valued and mirrored. Also the counsellor should be attentive to a client's negative internal self-experiences (e.g. of being no good, bad, worthless etc.). A self object is very similar to the cognitive notion of self-schema as we shall see in chapter 3, except that a self object experience is more emotional.

*Idealizing:* This relates to the fact that the child needs to rely on others. When those to whom the child looks up to respond with helping and caring responses, the child feels soothed, secure and loved and develops basic trust. When this is not the case, the child feels that there is no one there for them and is unable to feel soothed in the presence of strong affect. Subsequently, as an adult, the person might resort to various defensive measures (e.g. drinking) to try to sooth themselves when under stress rather than cope adaptively. They may be distrustful of the counsellor, expecting to be let down in some way.

In counselling, the counsellor can empathize with the needs of the client in his/her wish to have some strong other come to the rescue and make things better. Thus the counsellor can recognize a client's yearning for rescue, his/her fear of abandonment and aloneness and being beyond rescue, beyond help. Hence, if a client says 'Can you help me? I feel so desperate', the counsellor should not say 'Well, it's up to you', or throw it back. Rather, the counsellor should focus on a collaborative journey, recognizing the client's need for rescue. Possible responses are, 'I recognize your need for help. Let's look at your problems together and see what you find helpful. Now, what's been going through your mind?'

*Belonging:* This relates to a child's need to feel at one with others, part of a group rather than an outsider and cut off. Again a counsellor can empathize and recognize the yearning to belong to some group and feel part of some social situation.

*Depression*  Kohut's theory of depression is very well summed up by Deitz (1988). Basically, depression results when a client has lost the external inputs (e.g. relationships) or the internal positive dimensions of self-experience that maintain positive feelings about the self. The goal of counselling is to facilitate and develop contact with internal positive self objects (or in cognitive terms positive self-schemata and attitudes) that bring back or develop representations of self as having worth and being able, rather than those of being worthless and unable. Deitz (1988) notes that these ideas are similar to cognitive counsellors' notions of self-schemata.

In a way, Kohut's view of depression is that it is nearly always secondary to a painful sense of disappointment; disappointment that life has turned out the way it has; that others are not as loving or reliable as was hoped; that plans have not come to fruition and so on. Somehow one has not made it; a position portrayed so brilliantly in Arthur Miller's play, *Death of a Salesman* (for a further discussion of this see Baker and Baker, 1988). It is important to help the person articulate their sense of disappointment and to reflect on the sources of this disappointment, often of unrealistic aspirations, misinterpretations or unmet needs. In this theory, anger is secondary to feeling blocked and thwarted.

*The internal experience*   The counsellor attempts to make genuine contact with the depressed client's internal experiences. These can be of various forms, for example a sense of weakness, badness, shame, envy, fear, hopelessness, emptiness, and so forth. The idea that some of these experiences relate to unmet needs or punitive early experiences is helpful and Kohut's concepts allow us to be more focused in our empathy. It is through our empathic understanding and responses that a client is able to feel understood and recognized; no matter what technique one uses, if these are not provided then counselling may run into difficulties.

Some key issues of the therapeutic relationship are as follows:

---

Key issues 1.1   The therapeutic relationship

1 The counsellor recognizes the basic ingredients of a therapeutic relationship and how it differs from other forms of relationship.
2 The counsellor shows openness, genuineness and positive regard – and is nonjudgemental.
3 The counsellor attempts to become aware of the basic interpersonal needs of the depressed client in terms of mirroring, recognition, valuing and idealizing as experiences to be worked with and understood rather than ignored.
4 The counsellor recognizes the common experience of disappointment as part of the depression.
5 The counsellor attempts to create a 'safe place' for counselling to take place.
6 The counsellor offers time and space for exploring and the 'invitation' to talk.

---

*Empathy*

It is recognized that the counsellor should attempt to form an empathic relationship with the client, enabling the client to feel understood and accepted, and to explore painful feelings. However, there remains confusion over the nature of the empathic relationship as it can be mimicked in an automatic way and in this sense be non-genuine. Also, there are real misunderstandings about empathy. Common ones are errors in the distinctions between genuineness, unconditional positive regard and empathy. Consider two examples from Book (1988: 422).

*Example 1:*
A first-year resident, when verbally assaulted by a paranoid client,

responded, 'I'm glad to see you can get your anger out.' The client hesitated, looked perplexed, and then angrily roared, 'You bastard! To be so happy that I am this upset!' When asked about his comment, the resident stated, 'I was just trying to be empathic.'

In this example the counsellor had confused a genuine desire to help the patient feel safe to express his anger with empathy.

*Example 2:*
A Holocaust survivor raged against the rudeness to which he felt subjected at work. His Jewish counsellor responded, 'It really makes me angry when I hear that. What the hell's the matter with them?' The client responded, 'That's what I'm telling you. They're all a bunch of butchers.'

In the second example the counsellor was responding from his own frame of reference. Book gives many other examples of confusions between genuineness, unconditional positive regard and empathy, including hearing but not really believing that a client can mean what they say, or making subtle alterations in the client's statement that actually changes the meaning.

In empathy, one listens and attends to both what is actually said and expressed, and what is not. One notes possible hidden shame and resentment, the fear of loss or the disappointment that lies behind the self-attack. As Kohut (1977) points out, a client's rage can often hide a deep sense of loss, being devalued and marginalized. An empathic response helps the client make contact with those feelings and their internal self-judgements. Another misunderstanding of empathy is filling in the blanks or finishing a client's sentence for him/her. This can be experienced as an intrusion. Instead, the counsellor can respond so as to help the client fill in his/her own blanks. Thus, as Book (1988) says, empathy may be understanding what the client is going to say, but being empathic is not saying it. A good measure of empathy is whether or not it enables clients to deepen their understanding and continue with their narrative.

A genuine empathic response from the counsellor is not necessarily perceived as such by the client, and therefore Miller (1989) refers to the 'therapeutic empathic communication process'. This is a five-stage model involving a counsellor's recognition of the client's internal experience (via the client's verbal and nonverbal cues), the sending of signals of recognition, and the client's ability to recognize and internalize such signals (i.e. I understand. I show you I understand, and you understand that I have understood). Empathy is a way of being with or an 'in-tuneness to' the client, not simply a skill to be 'brought to bear'. As Margulies (1984)

Table 1.1    *Distinctions between sympathy and empathy*

| Sympathy | Empathy |
| --- | --- |
| Involves a heightened awareness of the suffering or need of the other. Something to be alleviated. The focus is on the other person's well being. | Involves a heightened awareness of the experiences of the other (not necessarily suffering) as something to be understood. |
| Behaviour is on relating, acting for, alleviating (or mediating responses). | Behaviour is on knowing, conceptualizing, understanding. |
| Sympathy is relatively automatic and effortless. | Empathy is effortful and depends on imaginal capabilities. |
| In sympathy the self is moved by the other. | The self reaches out to the other. |
| The other is the vehicle for understanding and some loss of identity may occur. | The self is the vehicle for understanding and never loses its identity. |

points out, empathy requires a 'sense of wonder' and caring interest (Gilbert, 1989) in the client's story. Interest itself can appear detached; caring alone can involve sympathy.

*Sympathy and empathy*    There is no clear evidence that sympathy at times is not helpful, but empathy is regarded as the more helpful. Thus it is beneficial to be clear about the differences. Table 1.1 outlines some of these differences.

Consider a client who is crying and giving strong signals of emptiness and loneliness. Our empathic feelings are close to how the client actually feels: empty, alone. Our sympathetic feelings are those that elicit the desire to touch the person, help alleviate the pain, to reassure them that it's going to be okay. In very emotional situations it can be quite difficult to recognize these differences. At times, sympathy is not necessarily anti-therapeutic and can be helpful, especially when blended with empathy in the form of compassion (Gilbert, 1989). However, the counsellor must be clear about the distinctions and not be carried away by feelings of the desire to rescue, which can break into the client's self-healing process and not match the client's needs. Key issues in empathy are as follows.

---

Key issues 1.2   Empathy

1 Empathy involves attentiveness to the verbal and nonverbal affective messages emanating from the client.
2 It is nonjudgemental.
3 It encourages exploration, especially of core areas and life themes and is sensitive to blocks and/or fears.
4 It is focused on knowing, understanding and sharing rather than helping, and alleviating (as in sympathy).
5 Empathy is reflective and thoughtful and involves effort, unlike sympathy which can be immediate, automatic and is relatively effortless.
6 It is flexible and avoids the client feeling 'pinned down or exposed'.

---

*Is empathy enough?*   Cognitive counsellors doubt that the qualities of accurate empathy, positive regard and genuineness are, by themselves, sufficient to produce change. Education into the way an individual thinks about events and labels or puts him/herself down is crucial for change. But cognitive counsellors do believe that these qualities are necessary ingredients of a helping relationship. Although works on cognitive counselling do not always stress the role of the therapeutic relationship (but see Dryden, 1989b), it is assumed that the counsellor is already proficient in these skills (Beck et al., 1979). Unfortunately, not enough attention has been given to these aspects.

Frank (1982) suggests that many states of depression and other conditions are the result of demoralization. A variety of approaches can reduce demoralization if they include such things as understanding, sharing, respect, interest, support, encouragement, acceptance, validation, forgiveness, education and even inspiration. Thus, a helping relationship may go far beyond the ingredients first noted by Rogers. Gilbert (1989, 1992) has pointed out that there are two fundamental systems in the brain – defence and safety. When individuals perceive threats, their actions and cognitions are self-defensive to avoid harm. Such actions tend to be automatic and rapid and reduce the chances of exploration. Safety involves such aspects as trust and confidence that the environment will not deliver threats. Safety increases exploration of and integration of material. Many depressed clients are highly attuned to threats (e.g. of losses, put-downs, rejections). The counsellor therefore tries to engage the safety system to allow exploration of painful material and begin to take the risks necessary for change. To a large degree psychopathology arises when the defence system is highly activated. Not enough attention has been given to these two fundamental systems.

*Counsellor skills*
There are various core skills that help the construction of a therapeutic relationship, especially the development of accurate empathy. These help convey a sense of being understood and cared for. They act as encouragements to the client to continue to explore and discover.

*Nonverbal behaviour*   We are only just beginning to research and explore the impact of nonverbal behaviour in counselling but it is probably profound. Facial expressions and body posture help to convey a sense of being with the client. Nonverbal behaviour helps to set the emotional climate of counselling and the conditions of warmth. One's style should be relaxed and welcoming but not too laid back and uninterested.

*Minimal encouragers*   Often clients only require prompts. These can be nonverbal, such as nods or other head and eye movements, or verbal prompts such as 'Hmm', 'Ah-ha', etc. Subtle prompts may call forth different types of information than more direct questions which can be controlling or directive. Sometimes it is useful to encourage exploration with simple words like, 'Because?', 'And?' or 'So?' This is short for 'this happened because . . .?', 'You see that as important because . . .?' (Nonverbal behaviour and voice intonation are important here: a 'so' can sound hostile rather than a position of interest.) These help the person to link ideas and allows the discussion to flow more naturally. At other times the counsellor can encourage exploration with more open questions 'Can we look at this more closely?', 'Can you say more about that?' Also, if the counsellor does not understand what the person is saying or meaning then it is helpful to say so, for example, 'I'm not sure I understand that, could you help me by explaining further', or 'Can we go into that a little?' etc.

*Open and closed questions*   Open questions leave the person to respond in their own way. For example, the classic cognitive question of 'What was going through your mind?' is an open question. Other examples are 'What did you make of that or how did that affect you?' Closed questions are aimed to elicit more specific information. 'Can you tell me how you are sleeping?', 'What is your sex life like?' Closed questions do not allow the client to articulate their own meanings and should be used very sparingly. Many novice counsellors are good at closed and directive questions but less skilled with open questions, the real bedrock of counselling.

*Reflecting feelings* Sometimes feelings are implicit in a message and the counsellor can draw attention to them. This requires attentiveness to the way a message is conveyed, for example:

> *Patient:* When Sally invited me in for a coffee after the dance I just had to turn her down. At that point I wanted to get home as quickly as possible.
> *Counsellor:* Sounds as if her offer made you pretty anxious.
> *Patient:* Absolutely. I found my stomach turn over in case she wanted me to stay the night and all.

However, the same statement given in a different way and in a different context may prompt a different reflection of feelings:

> *Patient:* When Sally invited me in for a coffee after the dance I just had to turn her down. At that point I wanted to get home as quickly as possible.
> *Counsellor:* Sounds as if her offer made you irritated.
> *Patient:* Absolutely. She knew I had a busy day the next day and that I was really tired and there she was making more demands on me.

Reflecting feelings enables the counsellor to convey his/her understanding and awareness of the client's internal view and experience. However, the cognitive counsellor would follow this up with a statement like 'So you thought that Sally was making demands on you.' The counsellor would be cautious not to reinforce the idea that it was Sally's request that produced the affect. Rather, the counsellor would direct attention to the client's interpretation of Sally's behaviour and that maybe this interpretation is open to an alternative view. Thus, although cognitive counsellors reflect feelings, they also attempt to make clear that it is the interpretation that is important in influencing the type of feelings a client may have.

*Paraphrasing* Paraphrasing also enables the counsellor to convey understanding, but here the focus is on content. This is not to be confused with simply repeating what the client has just said in parrot fashion (sometimes mistaken as an empathic response). Rather it is designed to show 'being with' the client and understanding the meaning in the message.

> *Patient:* After the relationship broke up my car went wrong so I was stuck at home and just had time to brood. The bills were piling up

and I've just put them on to one side. Now they are threatening to cut off my electricity. I just can't get things sorted out.

*Counsellor:* So your time to brood on the lost relationship has made it difficult for you to keep on top of things.

*Summarizing* Summarizing is similar to paraphrasing in its basic skill but takes larger chunks of meaning, follows long(er) periods of exploration, and focuses on a core theme(s), for example:

*Counsellor:* Given what you have been saying about your family and recent events you perceive that no one has shown much interest in your difficulties and this has led you to think that you are rather unimportant and uncared for.

Summarizing is used in many different ways. It is often used in taking a history and can be a form of crystallization, to help a client and counsellor focus on *recurrent patterns/themes of behaviour, events and styles of explanation for events.* It can also be used when the counsellor explores an inference chain (see chapter 3). It is useful to summarize frequently, to clarify with the client a shared understanding. Many novice counsellors do not summarize enough.

When we look in more detail at the cognitive model for depression it is important to keep in mind that cognitive counselling requires the counsellor, at the outset, to be proficient in these basic counselling skills of empathy, reflection of feelings, paraphrasing and summarizing. Practice and supervision are helpful to 'craft' these aspects and to understand and gain empathy for their use and timing in the sessions. However, it is the basic empathic concern that will help here rather than attempts to apply them mechanically (e.g. I must get in at least four minimal encouragers, a couple of paraphrases, and four or five summaries etc.).

### Getting it wrong

No one is perfect and often we can get it wrong. We make an intervention that seems to change or interrupt the flow of the dialogue and the client becomes silent or looks away. Such nonverbal signals are important to note. Sometimes a simple acknowledgement or even apology is helpful.

*Counsellor:* I note that when I said [. . .] that you were silent and looked away. Maybe I misunderstood you. Did anything go through your mind just now?

We can now summarize the core skills in counselling:

Key issues 1.3   Core skills

1 Attentiveness to verbal and nonverbal behaviours in both counsellor and client.
2 Attendant behaviour of listening and observing.
3 Minimal encouragers.
4 Reflecting feelings.
5 Paraphrasing.
6 Open and closed questions.
7 Summarizing.
8 Awareness of therapeutic ruptures and the (nondefensive) reparation process.

## A model of helping

Most counsellors require a model of helping that will act as their road map of progress. Here is an outline that is suitable for cognitive-interpersonal counselling.

1 Making contact with the client and enabling the client to express him/herself and tell his/her story.
2 Making an effort to form an 'empathic connection' with the client and see through his/her eyes, how it is for him/her now.
3 Enabling the client to comprehend 'being recognized and heard', and that the counsellor is attempting to make an empathic connection; the counsellor is trying to understand 'it' from the client's point of view, how it feels inside, the depth of despair, the hopelessness, the fear and the sense of failure/shame, the feelings of unmet needs (i.e. counselling is not technique-focused irrespective of the client's actual feelings).
4 Offering a coherent, understandable approach to working with internal experiences and social behaviours. This involves enabling the client to understand and be a collaborative partner in the process of counselling. In this respect cognitive counsellors differ radically from the non-educational approaches. Their basic belief is that the more clients understand the nature of their distress and can learn what they can do to change and cope, the sooner they will recover and the less likely they are to relapse.
5 Developing a working therapeutic alliance that enables the client to become open to new experiences (e.g. in counselling) and to become more explorative.
6 Engaging the client to move, take risks, rework past losses and form new insights and new conceptualization for experience. Forming shared goals.

7 Working with blocks to change and facilitating 'the hard work' for change.

8 Developing resistance to future depression by (for example) learning not to self-attack but to respect the self as a fallible human being.

## Concluding comments

Depression can be a very serious condition which may sometimes end in suicide. The depressed client can have serious effects on his/her children and family relationships, in addition to the misery the client endures. More than anything else the depressed client's internal experience needs to be understood and an empathic connection made such that he/she can gain hope (break up demoralization) and begin the work of rebuilding his/her life. But there is more to counselling than understanding and empathizing. The cognitive-interpersonal approach requires the counsellor to be in tune with basic concepts of interpersonal relationships and also to be aware of techniques for challenging negative beliefs. In the next chapter we explore styles and forms of interpersonal behaviour.

## 2

## Interpersonal Dimensions of Depression

There have been many different theories of the causes of depression (see Gilbert, 1992 for a review). Over the past two decades, social relationships have been shown to play an important role in the cause, maintenance and recovery of depression. In a seminal work, Brown and Harris (1978) found that in a community sample of women, depression was often associated with vulnerability factors (such as low self-esteem and low intimacy with spouse) and provoking agents (such as various losses and threats that have long-term consequences). They suggest that events that reduce a person's sense of value and self-esteem are particularly important in depression (see also chapter 8 of this volume, and Brown, 1989, for an update of this work). Indeed, many theories of depression regard self-esteem as a central aspect of depression (Becker, 1979). Working with attitudes to the self will therefore be a central focus of this book.

Klerman et al. (1984) developed the interpersonal approach to treating depression. They emphasized the role of (social) life events, the nature of significant relationships (mostly in the present, but also with some consideration of early relationships), the interpersonal behaviours a person uses to gain and maintain relationships and resolve conflicts. This model proposes various specific causes of depression: grief and loss, interpersonal role transitions, role conflicts and social skills deficits. The model outlines various therapeutic interventions for dealing with each source of difficulty. Cognitive counsellors also believe that it is our attitudes and beliefs concerning important relationships that are often the focus of therapeutic intervention (Beck et al., 1979).

Beck (1967) suggested that many of the styles of thinking that are associated with depression arise from early experience with parents and others. Early acquired negative beliefs may not be observable when a person is well. They are latent but can be activated by life events. Over recent years there has been development of these ideas and an effort to gain a clearer understanding of how our early relationships shape adult styles of relating. Thus, interpersonal-cognitive counselling explores some of the origins of these early beliefs, how they are activated in the present, become amplified in depression and how a client can begin to change them. Recently, cognitive counsellors have begun to utilize concepts from attachment theory to help formulate client problems.

## Attachment theory

There is a large body of evidence that early relationships with parental figures, siblings and friends result in the development of internal working models of relationships (Bowlby, 1973, 1980; Guidano and Liotti, 1983; McCann et al., 1988; Safran and Segal, 1990). An internal working model is a set of basic ideas, beliefs and expectations about the self and about others, and typical styles of interaction. For example, I may have a working model that people in authority will always try to force me to do what they want and that I have to comply. Or I might have an internal working model that I need other people to love and approve of me but others are unreliable and rejecting. In cognitive terms these are called basic schemata (see chapter 3).

Attachment theory argues that we have an innate predisposition to form attachment relationships. Indeed, without care and protection an infant cannot survive. Bowlby (1980) and others have suggested it is common, in the history of a depressed person, to find various distortions in early attachment relationships which produce dysfunctional internal working models of relationships. Bowlby outlines three types of early experience which predispose to helplessness and depression:

(a) He is likely to have had the bitter experience of never having attained a stable and secure relationship with his parents despite having made repeated efforts to do so, including having done his utmost to fulfil their demands and perhaps also the unrealistic expectations they may have had of him. These childhood experiences result in his developing a strong bias to interpret any loss he may later suffer as yet another of his failures to make or maintain a stable affectional relationship.

(b) He may have been told repeatedly how unlovable, and/or how inadequate, and/or how incompetent he is. Were he to have these experiences they would result in his developing a model of himself as unlovable and unwanted, and a model of attachment figures as likely to be unavailable, or rejecting or punitive. Whenever such a person suffers adversity therefore, so far from expecting others to be helpful he expects them to be hostile and rejecting.

(c) He is more likely than others to have experienced actual loss of a parent during childhood . . . with consequences to himself that, however disagreeable they might have been, he was impotent to change.

Such experiences would confirm him in the belief that any effort he might make to remedy his situation would be doomed to failure. (Bowlby, 1980: 247–8)

Bowlby links these early learning experiences with the development of various predispositions for interpreting information in a negative way. As a result of our early experiences of attachment relationships, research suggests that there are four basic interpersonal styles that emerge in childhood and are carried through into later, adult life. Some of these result in major difficulties in adjusting to loss, role conflicts, and role transitions later in life. These styles have recently been outlined by Collins and Read (1990).

*Secure attachment:* These individuals are able to get close to others or cope with distance. They are comfortable with depending on others and with others depending on them and rarely worry, in the normal course of events, about abandonment or getting too close and intimate. They have a basic trust in themselves and in others. In counselling they develop trust fairly easily, are open, but also recognize boundaries.

*Anxious ambivalent attachment:* These individuals feel that they cannot get close enough to others and are very sensitive to cues of rejection or abandonment. They often worry that their partners and friends may leave them or ignore them. Their needs for constant reassurance of their lovability and acceptance sometimes drives others away and can show up as clinginess, possessiveness, jealousy and other anxious forms of attachment and relating. They are more likely to be emotionally expressive.

*Avoidant attachment:* These individuals prefer distance and are uncomfortable if others get too close. They do not like to be dependent on others nor for others to be dependent on them. They often find that their partners wish for them to be closer but this call to intimacy is frightening to them. They are often distrustful of others' motives and are sensitive to being hurt and/or controlled in relationships. They are the least emotionally expressive and may be subject to strong shame. Recent work suggests that shame is a strong developmental affect that significantly influences subsequent relationship styles (Schore, 1991).

*Ambivalent attachment:* These individuals show mixtures and oscillations of anxious and avoidant. If others get too close they are worried about being controlled and 'swamped' and show avoidant patterns. If others are too distant they are worried about abandonment and aloneness and show anxious patterns. In borderline clients this oscillation can be marked.

These styles may be acted out in the counselling situation, i.e. some depressed patients appear anxious and needy, others are withdrawn, distant or hostile, yet others oscillate between these two styles. Gilbert (1989, 1992) has outlined how often our social behaviour either relates to self-defensive and protection needs or arises from feeling safe and explorative with others. The defence and safety systems are major mediators of affects. Guidano and Liotti (1983), Liotti (1988) and Safran and Segal (1990) have explored how early attachment relationships have powerful effects on various, basic self–other beliefs and relational style, and influence the experience of connectedness and relatedness with others. These styles are useful to note because, when counselling a depressed person, they can be re-enacted during counselling. For example, a client who has an ambivalent style may move between appearing needy and dependent, to being aloof and distant, or angry. Some of the key issues for the counsellor interested in attachment theory are given below:

---

Key issues 2.1   Attachment relations

1 Early attachment relationships play a central role in forming internal working models about self and about others.
2 When a client becomes depressed, different types of attachment relations may become prominent or exaggerated and these can be enacted in the counselling relationship and outside it.
3 At present there appear to be four basic patterns of attachment relationships: secure, anxious, avoidant and ambivalent.
4 The counsellor should be aware that different depressed clients will have different interpersonal styles. Some will want to be very close and cared for, while others will stay distant and aloof, yet others will oscillate between closeness and distance.

---

Attachment theory tends to focus on close relationships. However, there are various forms of relationships that we can have with others, such as work relationships and friendly relationships. These roles may become central to our plans, hopes and expectations for the future. If the enactment of these roles is frustrated or blocked we may become depressed because we lose an important source of self-valuing and self-esteem (Brown and Harris, 1978). This is the central idea in the work of two researchers, Oatley and Boulton (1985). Another approach to social roles has been from evolution theory (Gilbert, 1989, 1992). This approach explored care-eliciting behaviour, care-giving behaviour, cooperative behaviour and competitive behaviour and how different people are sensitive to failure in these various roles. From this approach depression is seen to arise from the experience of powerlessness.

We all have different internal working models of relationships that allow us to enact certain types of social behaviour (for example, elicit care, help and support from others, form friendships or compete with others). In the next section we look at some of the common, socially focused schemata of self–other relationships.

## Depressive schemata

There are some typical self–other schemata that are common in depression. Clients bring with them into counselling a history of how they have come to understand themselves in relation to others. Sometimes these schemata may have been latent but become activated due to life events (Beck, 1967). Many researchers have outlined various basic interpersonal schemata in depression, including: approval; achievement; self-worth; efficacy/entrapment; affect; and power.

### Approval

The need for approval in depression is well recognized in cognitive counselling (Burns, 1980; Beck, 1983). Arieti and Bemporad (1980a,b) offer the clearest exposition of people with strong approval schemata:

> They do not experience satisfaction directly from effort but only through an intermediary, who gives or withholds rewards. They have formed an imagined agreement with the important other that may be called a bargain relationship . . . in which the individual foregoes the independent derivation of gratification in return for the continuance of nurturance and support of the esteemed other. This pattern of relating was initiated by the parent during the childhood of the predepressive individual but in later life the individual will reinstate similar relationships in a transferential manner. Other characteristics of this type of depressive personality are clingingness, passivity, manipulativeness and avoidance of anger. These character traits may be seen as the means by which the individual attempts to extract support from the needed other as well as to ensure continuation of the relationship. (Arieti and Bemporad, 1980a: 1360–1)

Beck (1983) calls these types sociotropic. The psychoanalytic writers Blatt et al. (1982) refer to them as anaclitic, while existential theorists (e.g. Yalom, 1980) call these styles the pursuit of the ultimate rescuer. In attachment theory these would be anxious attachment styles. Arieti and Bemporad (1980a,b) emphasize the failure to individuate and develop autonomy.

Key beliefs of self include: I need stronger others on whom I can rely; I am nothing or empty without love; life is meaningless without a close relationship(s).

## Achievement

Achievement types attempt to ward off beliefs of personal inadequacy and depression by obtaining lofty goals. Some may have a more chronic form of personality difficulty characterized by many taboos (e.g. on pleasure). Arieti and Bemporad (1980a) outline the characteristics of these individuals as follows:

> These individuals invest their self-esteem in the achievement of some lofty goal and shun any other activities as possibly diverting them from this quest. Originally, achievement was rewarded by the parents, and so high marks for some outstanding performance was sought as a way to ensure support and acceptance. In time, the individual selects some fantastic goal for himself which he then pursues frantically, apparently for its own sake. However, closer scrutiny reveals that the achievement of this goal is burdened with surplus meaning. The individual believes that the goal will transform his life and, possibly, himself. Attaining his desired objective will mean that others will treat him in a special way or that he will finally be valued by others. Just as the dominant other type of depressive individual uses fantasies of the relationship to derive a feeling of worth, the dominant goal type of depressive individual obtains meaning and esteem from fantasies about obtaining his objective. Both types also use these fantasies to eschew ratification or meaning from other activities in everyday life. In contrast to the 'dominant other' type, this form of depressive personality is usually seclusive, arrogant and often obsessive. In addition, this form of personality organization is commonly found in men. . . . (Arieti and Bemporad, 1980a: 1361)

In other types of theory these would be seen as narcissistic vulnerabilities. They are aimed at following a strategy of gaining approval and respect via achievement (Gilbert, 1992). Although they may deny they wish to be dominant, the fantasies of such people show that this is often the issue. In one case the person felt that, as the second child, his parents would rather he had been a girl. His older brother did well at school and in a subsequent career, whereas he felt he was a disappointment to his parents. Much of his striving had been to try to do something which his family and others would recognize, and on which they would bestow high respect and status.

Key beliefs are: I must succeed and be recognized as having done so; life is meaningless without a clear goal; achievement is the way people are measured; without success, I am a failure.

## Self-worth

Gilbert (1984, 1992) suggests that self-worth schemata are related to our basic beliefs that we have something to contribute to the world. We derive a sense of self-worth in childhood from the attention, reinforcement and praise bestowed on us by parents, teachers and others. Thus self-worth is often related to ideas of being worthy of, and therefore deserving of something, e.g. praise, attention, love and so forth. This is a complex point related to our biological predispositions and our need to appear attractive, able and talented to others and elicit their investment (see Gilbert, 1992, for a detailed discussion of investment theory and self-schemata). A typical depressive self-worth belief is, 'I have nothing of value to contribute to a relationship, group or even society at large.' As pointed out elsewhere (Gilbert, 1984), some people can lose a sense of self-worth because they do not feel that they are reinforcing to others. When the lover ends the relationship the message is, 'You are no longer reinforcing enough for me to wish to continue.' Many depressions are ignited by similar discoveries of interpersonal losses (e.g. loss of a confiding relationship, Brown and Harris, 1978).

## Efficacy/entrapment

Efficacy beliefs and schemata are also central in depression. Seligman (1975, 1989) showed how a perception of helplessness leads to depression. Here the basic schemata are, 'I am ineffective and have little control. Nothing I do can work.' These basic beliefs not only affect self-esteem but give a negative view of the future, leading to hopelessness (Abramson et al., 1989).

Related to perceptions of self-efficacy is opportunity, especially opportunities to change situations. Sometimes a key theme in depression is a perceived lack of opportunity which can be experienced as entrapment. Entrapment may involve being in a relationship, whether intimate (e.g. a marriage, family) or social–public (e.g. work), that one cannot get away from. For example, a person would like to leave their neglectful or abusive spouse but for economic reasons, guilt, fear of the spouse's reaction or fear of aloneness they are unable to leave. Thus they feel they have little control over their future and feel trapped. A sense of being stuck in an undesirable situation and not being able to move from it is more common in depression than is sometimes recognized. Thoughts and feelings of entrapment and hopelessness are often associated with suicidal intent.

*Affect*
Depressed clients may have many kinds of negative emotions that can be the source of confusion. A person's own internal feelings can be a source of negative self-judgement. Strong feelings of rage, envy and shame (which are socially focused) can activate negative self-schemata. Typical depressive beliefs are 'My feelings are beyond my control' or 'My negative feelings are bad and evidence of a bad, weak, inferior or unlovable self. Therefore to feel good about myself I must repress, control or conceal these feelings.' Negative affects can act like internal stimuli that cue negative self-experience (Gilbert, 1992), a point long held by cognitive counsellors. Of course, it is not only negative affects that can be a source of negative self-judgements. For example, a client felt strong sexual attraction to a man at work and thought that this was sinful.

Sometimes, emotions and memories can be poorly integrated into consciously available schemata. Thus the counsellor may need to help the client avoid emotional repression by focusing on the meaning and experiences of affect, especially as it occurs during counselling (Greenberg and Safran, 1987).

*Power*
Our internal sense of social power is related to three basic judgements. The first is social comparison. There are two types of social comparison, *superior–inferior* and *same–different* (Gilbert, 1992). Depressives often make negative social comparisons in both domains, that is they feel both different from others and inferior (Brewin and Furnham, 1986; Swallow and Kuiper, 1988). Key beliefs might be: 'Others are more able, better, nicer than I. Therefore I must conceal my weakness and differences to avoid rejection and hurt.'

The second aspect, related to social comparison, is dominance. Beliefs in personal inferiority can lead to inhibited, submissive behaviour, shame and envy, or desires to excel and compensate for an underlying sense of weakness/inferiority. A sense of being in a one-down position and under the control of others can arise from abusive or neglectful relationships. A sense of inferiority and weakness activates internal inhibition and reduces explorative behaviour (Gilbert, 1992).

The third aspect relates to approval seeking and is a form of excessive accommodation to others. The basic belief here is 'In order to be loved and avoid abandonment I must accommodate myself to the other – be for them what they want me to be.' Clearly this limits the degree to which a person can feel free to express his/her own needs, preferences and desires in the relationship. This choice of inhibition of self often results in feelings of inferiority, a loss of power and limits assertive behaviour.

---

Key issues 2.2 Depressive schemata

1 Depressive schemata often relate to basic self-beliefs.
2 Various schemata involved in depression are: approval, achievement, self-worth, efficacy/entrapment, affect and power.
3 For each type of schemata there are three issues: how people judge themselves, how they judge others and how, as a consequence of these judgements, they feel and behave.
4 Schemata help to organize social behaviour and relationship style. For example, believing one is inferior to others may lead to inhibited and cautious social behaviour.

---

## Love and power in self-relationships

As we will see, a central focus in cognitive counselling, especially for depression, is concerned with how people rate and judge themselves. Leary (1957) suggested that there are two central dimensions for making these (inter)personal judgements: love–hate and dominant–subordinate (power). Individuals can take up various roles with others in terms of the degree of love and power they give or withhold from self and others. Thus I may give love and acceptance to others but be very hostile and non-accepting to myself. Or I may be very accepting of myself but be very condemning of others (for a review of these concepts see Duke and Nowicki, 1982; Birtchnell, 1990; and, in regard to counselling, Horowitz and Vitkus, 1986).

The idea that we can take attitudes to ourselves that are either hostile and down-putting (e.g. self-downing) or nurturing and facilitating is important. In many forms of depression one finds that the internal attitudes to self, that is the relationship we have with ourselves, is hostile and down-putting. Gilbert (1989) has pointed out that the way we can understand self–other relationships can also be a way we understand ourselves. Part of the role of the counsellor is to help the client (a) to recognize the degree and extent of internal self-downing and negative self-talk (e.g. I'm a failure, I'm boring, I'm useless); and (b) to change this negative self-talk to a more nurturing and accepting self-talk and self-relationship. This is achieved by teaching a client to recognize and avoid self-labelling, and extreme and global self-evaluations (see chapter 4). It is not only via the cognitive behavioural challenges that this is achieved but also via basic therapeutic skills and the relationships established.

*Weakness/badness and self-criticism*
In any one case these basic styles will be more or less prominent, though in different patterns. Greenberg and colleagues have indicated, however, that there appear to be two aspects of internal self-relationship that often come together to produce depression:

> Based on our clinical observation, it appears that depression is much more likely if a person's weak/bad, hopeless, self-organisation is triggered, than if the critical self and negative cognitions alone are activated. It is much more the person's response to the negative cognitions and their inability to cope with the self-criticisms, than the cognitions and criticisms alone, that lead to depression. People are unable to counter or combat the negative cognitions when the weak/bad helpless state has been evoked. This is when depressed affect emerges.
>
> It is thus the combination of the hostility of the critic and the activation of the weak/bad self which constitutes the experiential vulnerability to depression, and it may well be that the hostility is the crucial variable in invoking the weak/bad organisation. The weak/bad organisation, although it is a recurrent, possible self-organisation and therefore possesses some degree of structuralization, does not predominate in the person's every day functioning and is not necessarily accessible under normal circumstances. Other forms of self-organisation develop and help the person function in the world. (Greenberg et al., 1990: 170)

Thus, however people relate to their social worlds, depression is concerned with those schemata we discussed above, especially the issues of inferiority, negative self–other comparison, low self-efficacy and evaluations of entrapment (Gilbert, 1992). There are many reasons why a person may self-down and self-criticize. Sometimes it is a self-protective strategy to avoid punishment from others. Driscoll (1989) has outlined twelve different forms of what he calls self-condemnation. Each has a different therapeutic focus.

*Rescue of the self?*
In recent years there has been increasing interest in the role of the self in psychopathology, and there are many theories that help us to conceptualize it. In Kohut's self psychology the concept of self object (Wolf, 1988) has some overlap with self-schemata (Gilbert, 1992), although in self psychology it is more closely related to affective experience. Others (Oatley and Boulton, 1985) have stressed the importance of social roles and self-worth in plans and

expectancies in depression. Yet others discuss self-efficacy (Bandura, 1977). All these formulations speak to the internal experience of the self as it relates to both an inner world of feelings and an external world of events.

Many of these therapies suggest an important aspect to treatment, that is, to ensure that the self is supported. Counselling involves creating a safe environment that facilitates exploration of both internal experiences and new coping and social behaviours. Thus going too quickly into negative feelings of rage or envy before a good therapeutic relationship is established (a non-safe environment), or if the counsellor has not ascertained that the client can cope with these internal experiences without launching a savage attack on the self, is not helpful. For example, a man had great difficulties in coming to terms with grief over loss of his mother but had a highly idealized view of her (although in reality she sounded rather emotional, needy and neglectful). However, until he had reduced his self-critical attitudes and changed his self-attacking style, he was unable to deal with the strong emotions aroused. He was too busy telling himself 'I shouldn't feel like this', or 'These feelings are bad, I must get rid of them.' Grief itself was seen as evidence of personal weakness. Hence there was little point in trying to work through the grief until he could come to accept his own feelings without putting himself down.

---

Key issues 2.3   Internal relationships

1 Humans can have basic attitudes and styles of thinking about themselves as well as other people.
2 In depression attitudes to the self are often hostile and self-critical.
3 A depressed person may attack him/herself for being weak, bad or incompetent.
4 A key step in counselling is therefore to recognize and dispute these negative self-judgements.
5 Reducing self-attacking allows for various aspects of experience to be worked through without these being used as further evidence of a bad or weak self.
6 In essence, the counsellor is attempting to alter the client's relationship with him/herself, that is, their self-relationship.

### Activating the social environment: social relationships and the self

Social relationships feed the self-concept. It is via our interaction with the social environment that our sense of self is built up (Brown and Harris, 1978). In depression, the social environment may activate negative experiences of, and attitudes to, the self. For example, we did not get the promotion or recognition we wish and our efforts are rejected. The love relationship, from which so much was hoped, folds. Our confidants to whom we turned and trusted turn out not to be available when we need them. In cognitive-interpersonal counselling these outcomes are not only distressing in themselves but may ignite negative self-experiences and attitudes in terms of loss of power, loss of self-worth, loss of efficacy and so forth. As a consequence, depression remains an internal experience where we feel cut off from others and unable to achieve long-term plans.

However, research has shown that from infancy onwards we are not passive responders to an active environment, but actually help to shape it. Thus various basic beliefs about the self and others may result in the environment acting in a certain way that will confirm our beliefs. For example, a jealous person is so demanding of evidence of loyalty that eventually the partner tires and leaves, thereby confirming the person's basic belief of the untrustworthiness of lovers. A man believes that he has to control others and trust is dangerous. He is rather aggressive at work. When he gets into difficulty he finds that few are interested in helping him. This strengthens his belief that others are untrustworthy and uncaring. Thus life is a process of forming models and schemata of the world, acting as if these are true and eliciting certain kinds of feedback from the environment that (often) confirm our schemata. This is outlined in figure 2.1.

The interpersonal-cognitive counsellor may focus on the interpersonal behaviours that a client is enacting. The client-counsellor relationship often allows this sequence to be observed (that is, schemata – interpersonal (role) behaviour – social/environmental responses – schemata maintenance or amplification). Thus the client behaves in certain ways which invite certain responses from the counsellor or others and these in turn may be such to confirm the client's schemata. Many of these enactments affect the relationship via transference and counter-transference experiences. Watkins (1989a,b) offers an excellent overview of these issues.

To emphasize these points we can explore some recent examples. Stephen had strong moral views that one should not impose ideas

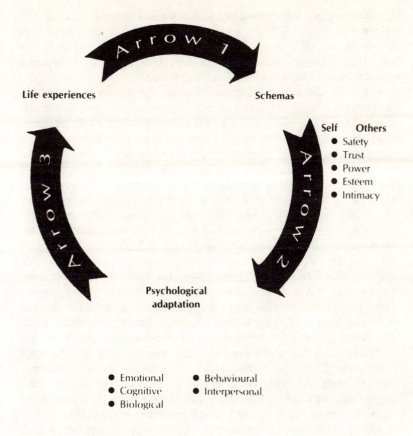

Figure 2.1   *The relation among life experiences, schemas and psychological adaptation (from McCann et al., 1988: 559).*

or needs on others. He was also anxious about rejection. Thus he had difficulty in making requests of others and tended to try to give hints to them hoping they would pick up on his needs. This was a particular problem when it came to dating women because he held back on giving signals of his attraction to potential lovers. He was not able to present himself as 'keen and interested'. Thus various possibilities went unexplored and by his own account he tended to be a 'background person'. The outcome was that in reality he presented himself as overly shy, rather boring, and was often ignored in social situations. In other words, Stephen appeared unenthusiastic, rarely sent signals of positive reinforcement to others and was 'hard work' in social situations. Thus he relied on the initiations of others. Eventually his loneliness and anger at feeling left behind lead to a serious suicide attempt. His internal models of self and others had the effect of eliciting certain kinds of response from his social world which reinforced his negative schemata of himself. He also felt envious of others and disliked people who were 'more pushy'.

Dora wanted to have a close relationship with a man. Unfortunately, confident men made her feel anxious and inferior and she avoided them. She thus tended to make relationships with unconfident men of low self-esteem. These relationships rarely lasted as the men frequently had problems in emotionally relating to her.

Marj had been placed in a caring role early in life due to parental illness. In her relationship with her husband she saw herself as the strong one and the one who always stayed calm. When talking about her husband's angry outbursts she would (with pride) tell how she would stay calm and tell him that he was making mountains out of molehills and to leave things to her. If he got irritated with her she would simply walk away and tell him to stop being childish. She failed to understand how this irritated him even more. In the day hospital she presented as a very competent person interested in others, full of advice but not really dealing with her own emotional pain and loneliness, which most often she denied. In reality, she was far from empathic of others. People found her intensely irritating. Unfortunately, she lacked insight into how her 'caring' behaviour was often controlling, and she remained aloof when it came to talking about her own feelings of emptiness. Thus again, although she wanted to be close and to feel that she was of value to others, in fact she elicited hostility and rejection.

Coyne (1976a,b) presented a model of depression which suggested that the depressed person is unattractive to others and therefore tends to elicit aversive responses. In this way a depression can be maintained. Depressed people initiate fewer positive interactions (e.g. going to a film, out to see friends, or sex), in part because they see it as too much effort. Not surprisingly, then, many marriages involving a depressed person are marked by a good deal of hostility (Gotlib and Colby, 1987; Beach et al., 1990). For both partners marriage can be seen as a trap as much as a source of support.

Thus, via our role relationships, we can 'activate' the environment into presenting us with certain types of responses. In cognitive-interpersonal counselling this is often a focus – to enable clients to understand how, at times, they are eliciting the very reactions from others that they complain of.

Nevertheless, many individuals can be on the receiving end of a good deal of hostility or neglect which they *do not* elicit, and in these cases the problem is more one of entrapment. So counsellors have to be aware that this is a complex area, and the comments here should not be taken to mean that depressed patients cause their own problems.

---

Key issues 2.5 Interpersonal working

1 Many depressions revolve around interpersonal issues.
2 The counsellor can become aware of how the client's interpersonal styles are often brought into the counselling setting (e.g. anxious, attachment or avoidant).
3 The counsellor can pay particular attention to the basic themes in depression (e.g. approval, achievement, self-worth, efficacy/entrapment, affects and power).
4 The counsellor can explore with the client how his/her behaviour may activate the environment to respond in ways that are undesirable.
5 The counsellor explores and clarifies with the client basic interactions between self and environment: schemata – interpersonal (role) behaviour – social/environmental responses – schemata maintenance or amplification.

---

**Concluding comments**

Cognitive-interpersonal counselling utilizes all the basic propositions of the cognitive approach. There is a focus on the construction of meaning via attributions, attitudes and so forth. The interpersonal dimension focuses on the early origin of self–other beliefs and increasingly is making links with attachment theory on the one hand and social psychology on the other (Gilbert, 1992). There is concern with how various beliefs result in social behaviour which in turn can act to confirm negative beliefs. These aspects are explored in the current situation of the client's relationship with the counsellor and other significant individuals in the client's life. Thus an understanding of interpersonal behaviour is important. With this brief introduction into social relationships we can now move to an exploration of the cognitive model.

# 3
## Cognitive Models of Helping and Change for Depressed Clients

Counselling relationships have key aspects to their process. For example, there is (a) *the bond* formed between the counsellor and client; (b) *the goals* and objectives of the counselling process; and (c) *the tasks* and activities carried out by the counsellor and the client to reach desired goals (Dryden, 1989c). As part of this process, counselling relationships pass through certain stages. Egan (1990) has outlined a general model for counselling which is also applicable to a cognitive approach. These stages include:

*The present scenario:* this is the first stage in the counselling process. Here the counsellor focuses on the basic tasks of inviting the client to tell his/her story, gaining insight into current difficulties and developing an appropriate relationship.

*The preferred scenario:* this marks the second stage. Here the counsellor negotiates and clarifies the goals, aims and objectives of counselling with the client.

*Getting there:* this is the third stage in the counselling process. Here the counsellor and client focus on the tasks of achieving the goals and objectives that have been agreed, and moving towards termination.

Each of these stages may be further subdivided, taking into account such things as resistances and blocks to change. The cognitive model moves through these stages with a particular focus on the interpretations, evaluations and beliefs of clients. The cognitive model argues that it is the personal meanings of events which are the key focus in counselling. For example, separation or divorce may be seen as a relief to one person, yet as a serious blow to self-esteem and future plans to another.

Cognitive counselling focuses on our thoughts and styles of interpretation of the (social) environment and social events, and also the implications we derive about ourselves. For example, 'Mary does not want to go out with me any more (event). This is because she does not like me any more (interpretation). This means

I am unlovable (self-judgement) and can never be happy' (future self-judgement).

There are three basic concepts in cognitive counselling comprising:

1 Automatic thoughts: these are the immediate ideas and interpretations that spring to mind. In depression they are often self-evaluative and carry implications for the future.
2 Rules for living and basic attitudes: these are the ideas and beliefs that guide our lives and set us in particular styles of living (e.g. I must be successful; I must be approved of). Basic attitudes are not always easily accessible and the client may hardly be aware of them.
3 Self–other schemata: these represent internal organization systems that form the basis of our self-judgements and experiences on the one hand, and our judgements and experiences of other people on the other. Cognitive therapists sometimes use the terms 'beliefs' and 'schemata' interchangeably.

## Automatic thoughts

Automatic thoughts, as the name implies, are those interpretations/ideas/thoughts that seem to come automatically to mind; they are our pop-up thoughts. They are the immediate, consciously available thoughts, require little or no effort and seem plausible. They are not arrived at through reflective reasoning. In depression they are often self-evaluative and future directed. Automatic thoughts are not necessarily in clear/syntactic language and can be poorly formulated, using fragments of grammar. Also it is common for them to occur in images or inner scenes, daydreams or fantasies (Gilbert, 1992). For example, the lover who does not phone at night as expected may lead a person to fantasize about the possibility that the lover is out with someone else. They may construct scenarios of seeing the lover in some particular place (e.g. a pub) and imagine him/her having a good time, laughing, drinking etc. We may enter into (internal) dialogue as a result of our automatic thoughts and fantasies. For example, having decided that the lover is out having a good time we may start to rehearse in our minds an argument or what we intend to say the next time they do phone. We may even rehearse something that we know in reality we would not carry out due to fear of being rejected/disliked, or because of moral concerns.

Sometimes we may not be fully aware of our automatic thoughts but experience only affect. For example, when the telephone does not ring we may find ourselves becoming more sad or irritated, but our awareness of our thinking may be hazy or poorly recognized. Hence, the depressed person may need to train themselves to attend to automatic thoughts so as to sharpen their focus and make them subject to more detailed analysis, communication and challenge. Their most salient aspect is their *core of meaning*. An important procedure of cognitive counselling is therefore to explore the immediate thoughts, teach how to recognize these thoughts as they occur and how to challenge them (e.g. Beck et al., 1979; Trower et al., 1988; Fennell, 1989; Blackburn and Davidson, 1990).

Another aspect involves the search for some underlying, deeper meaning or more global or extreme evaluations and beliefs. One of the most common forms of exploration to achieve this is called inference chaining or laddering. This technique is one of *guided discovery* and not interpretation.

### Inference chains

Inference chains are the ways our thoughts and interpretations are linked together. An inference chain follows an 'if A then B' form of reasoning. In other words, the client associates one idea or outcome with another. Usually a subsequent inference is more global, extreme and emotionally laden. For example: 'If my friend ignores me then it means he/she does not like me. This is because I am a boring person. If I am a boring person then I am unlovable. If I am unlovable I will never find a loving relationship and will be alone and depressed forever.'

The strength of the affect is often generated by the global evaluations at the end of the chain and the nature of these evaluations (i.e. this would be terrible and unbearable). Beck et al. (1979) suggest that there are particular types of distortions in the reasoning and automatic thoughts of depressed clients:

1 Arbitrary inference – drawing a negative conclusion in the absence of supporting data.
2 Selective abstraction – focusing on a detail out of context, often at the expense of more salient information.
3 Overgeneralization – drawing conclusions over a wide variety of things on the basis of single events.
4 Magnification and minimization – making errors in evaluating the importance and implications of events.
5 Personalization – relating external (often negative) events to the self when there is little reason for doing so.
6 Absolutistic, dichotomous thinking – thinking in polar opposites

(black and white). Something is all good, or totally bad and a disaster.

Others have added egocentric thinking, 'People must think the same way I do', and the telepathy error, 'People should know how I feel without me having to tell them.' Some of these 'errors' are not original to cognitive theory. For example, black and white thinking is called 'splitting' by object relations theorists. Also, it has become apparent that human reasoning in general often involves these styles of reasoning (Hollon and Kriss, 1984) and that depressed clients are not untypical in this. Content is more important.

The use of the word 'error' to describe these cognitive styles is unfortunate and has led to debate about whether or not clients are erroneous in their thinking; that is, the client is wrong and the counsellor is right. However, in some cases depressed people may actually be more accurate than nondepressed people (Taylor and Brown, 1988). There are many reasons a client may fall into a certain negative style of evaluation: life events, as a result of previous history and so forth. Also to suggest error is to suggest a correct way of thinking. These debates cloud the key issue of understanding meaning. Others have tried to overcome this problem with terms like dysfunctional versus functional/adaptive or 'goal securing' thinking. Thus, whether a thought is rational or not depends on whether it moves us closer to a desired goal. There are many philosophical problems with this view, however, thus it is preferable to talk in terms of depressing thoughts or anxious thoughts, etc. The main properties of automatic thoughts are given below.

---

Key issues 3.1 Automatic thoughts

1 They are triggered by events which may be external (e.g. criticism from another person) or internal (e.g. an affect).
2 They are immediately available and just jump or pop into the mind. Sometimes the client lacks awareness of them.
3 Thus they require little or no effort and appear to be spontaneous.
4 They occur in shorthand or images and are poorly formulated in language.
5 They follow no clear sequence as in logical reasoning or problem-solving.
6 They can be difficult to turn off, especially in the presence of emotional arousal.

7 They often seem plausible and reasonable to the client, although they may be far fetched (e.g. catastrophic).
8 They can arise in spite of evidence to the contrary.
9 They often follow certain styles (e.g. personalization, selective abstraction).

*Exploring automatic thoughts: inference chains*
As part of counselling one wants to help the client understand the links in his/her thoughts and beliefs and how these contribute to depression. This idea is not new. Rather, as Albert Ellis (e.g. Ellis and Whiteley, 1979) is fond of telling us, it was first described by the Stoic philosophers. They were very interested in the nature of subjective meaning: what is beauty?; what is honour?; what is justice?; what is evil? etc. There are no obvious scientific rules for deciding these things; therefore they believed that subjective meaning had to be open to discourse and discussion. To do this they derived what became known as the Socratic Method of Dialogue. This involved a style of questioning that sought to help identify the *criteria* people use to make subjective judgements.

Much of cognitive counselling should be understood from this perspective. It is not about 'retraining' in the sense that one might teach a dog new tricks. It is rather engaging with a person their internal constructions and meaning-making processes and helping them to explore alternatives, to treat *beliefs as hypotheses* and to test out ideas; to understand the relationship between thoughts (inner constructions, feelings and behaviours) and to acquire new skills. Although the basic procedures for explaining the cognitive model have been outlined elsewhere (Beck et al., 1979; Trower et al., 1988; Fennell, 1989; Blackburn and Davidson, 1990), for completeness a brief review needs to be outlined here.

In the first instance a person can be shown the cognitive model by using examples and highlighting the relationships among an event, a series of cognitions and a behavioural and emotional outcome. The counsellor may write down three columns A, B, C. A stands for an *Activating event*, B stands for *Beliefs* and C stands for *Consequences*. This is called the triple column technique.

| A | B | C |
|---|---|---|
| Activating event | Beliefs/appraisals Interpretations | Emotions Behaviour Biology |

The counsellor may then use the example of hearing a sound in one's kitchen at 2 am. First, the counsellor discusses various possibilities for the consequences, e.g. fear, anger, relief, etc. These are then written down together with the beliefs that would lead to the different emotions.

| A | B | C |
|---|---|---|
| Sound in kitchen at 2 am | It may be a thief. | Anxiety/fear |
| | It is my drunken spouse who has forgotten the key. | Anger |
| | It is my cat. | Calm |
| | It is my child home safely after a party. | Relief |

The counsellor may use this type of example to indicate how the interpretation of an event is associated with emotional, behavioural and biological changes. Two other areas should be discussed: context and history. Clearly, if one does not have a child then this cannot be part of the evaluation. Second, if someone has been abused then anxiety might become terror due to the activation of memory. Or if one's spouse is constantly coming home drunk then again memory is important.

Explanation of the cognitive model should be conducted in a friendly way and the use of gentle humour during the example sometimes helps to relax a client. It is important to check with the person that they see the validity of this approach. When this has been agreed the counsellor can then say, 'Okay, now let's use the same kind of approach to the kinds of problems you seem to be having. Can you give me an example of an event that has upset you in the past week. Right now, we are mainly interested to understand what this event meant for you.' This is then written down under A. The affects and behaviours elicited are written in column C. Then the counsellor says, 'Now let's look at what was going through your mind at B, to see if we can understand what leads to those feelings and behaviours at C' (Trower et al., 1988). When exploring an inference chain it should be conducted in the manner of a collaborative friendly venture; it is not an interrogation. The style of the interaction should be one of caring interest (Gilbert, 1989). The counsellor should avoid just 'firing off' questions, one after another, and intersperse questions with reflections and paraphrases. One tries to foster in the person a desire to explore and discover (*guided discovery*), yet also convey a sense of safety. Counsellors need to be sensitive to the current state of the client. For example, if a client has a desire to share painful feelings and be understood, has serious shame problems or is very inhibited, then there is little point doing highly focused work. The counsellor must be sensitive to these issues.

*Types of question*

Eliciting an inference chain is a kind of directed (as opposed to free) association. The cognitive counsellor is active and directive in the use of questions, and does not go beyond what has been said. To explore an inference chain requires a preparedness to suspend any effort to modify thoughts as the exploration unfolds. Some counsellors tend to jump in too quickly with their own interpretations or ideas, e.g. 'Do you think you are thinking this because . . .?;' or 'Isn't this because . . .?' and the counsellor engages in guessing. In cognitive exploration the counsellor tries not to suggest ideas but to let the person discover them for themselves. Cognitive counsellors believe that self-discovery works better than interpretation. Hence, the importance of the Socratic 'what' open question. The most basic questions are 'What went through your mind?' or 'What is going through your mind?' These are both examples of open questions which enable the client to focus more clearly and avoid vague descriptions of 'it', 'always', 'something'.

Other common questions are:

What would happen if . . .?
What would happen then/next?
What does that lead you to think/believe?
What conclusions do you draw from that?
What do you think this means?

To get at more specific self–other schemata:

What do you think other people thought?
What do you think was going through their minds?
What do you conclude about yourself?
What were you thinking about yourself?
What do you think they were thinking about you?
What were you thinking about you?

To work with historical data:

When was the first time you thought/felt this way and what was happening? (elicit images and memories).

Do you often have that view?
How often have you felt/thought this way?

As a rule of thumb 'what' questions encourage the person to explore the 'implications' of their thoughts/interpretations. The implications the counsellor is particularly interested in are those related to the pursuit of long-term goals and rules for living, idealizations, hopes and fears, and schemata of self and significant others. In other words, what does this thought or idea imply? One can also note the underlying theme, issues of shame and blocks to exploration.

Another form of questioning seeks to explore a more causal form of thinking. In this case the questions follow a 'why' set of questions, or less often a 'how' set of questions.

Why do you think that?
Why do you think that happened?
How do/did you reach that conclusion?
How do you think other people would see you because of that?
How do you think other people will react to you?

Although cognitive counsellors sometimes use 'why' questions, Egan (1990) argues that 'why' questions can be experienced as threatening. Thus they should be used cautiously or when you have established a good working relationship with the client. They are rarely used on the first interview.

Yet another set of questions seeks to enable clients to make predictions:

What are you likely to feel when you think this way?
What happens when you behave this way?
How do others respond to you when you behave this way?
What are the advantages and disadvantages of thinking/behaving this way?
What would be the advantages and disadvantages of making this change?

Helping clients predict the consequences of their ways of thinking, and predicting what would happen if they changed, is important in cognitive counselling as we shall see later. Again, it should be emphasized that the purpose of these kinds of questions is guided discovery – to give form and clarity to vagueness. Hence, the counsellor should be aware that sometimes clients may not actually answer the question but remain vague or answer a different question. Thus the counsellor wants to enable the client actually to focus on the question put. These questions are designed to help the client gain a clearer idea of what is going through his/her mind, the core essence of the meaning. They are not just to satisfy the curiosity of the counsellor.

To give an example: Jane was a depressed single parent who was trying to start a new relationship. However, she was cautious and doubtful of the person she was involved with and very attentive to cues of rejection.

*Counsellor:* Jane, you were saying that this weekend has been particularly bad for you. Can you remember any particular event that seemed to start it off?

*Jane:* I guess it was Friday night. Dave had said he would come over but then he phoned to say that he would not be able to make it as he had to go down to London to pick up some work.

*Counsellor:* How did you feel about that?

*Jane:* I was real disappointed and went to bed. I just switched off. Everything seemed pointless.

*Counsellor:* What went through your mind?

*Jane:* Hm . . . something like, here we go again. I am obviously not that important to him. He has better things to do. Maybe he would prefer not to be coming over.

*Counsellor:* So you thought he'd prefer not to come over. Did you have any thoughts about why that might be the case?

*Jane:* Yes. I got to thinking that maybe I am not really that much fun to be with. He probably thinks I am a rather boring person and does not want to get too involved with a single parent with kids. I began to think that sooner or later he would pull out of the relationship and I'd end up alone again.

*Counsellor:* I see, so when Dave didn't come over you began to think that there were things about you that he was rejecting, like being a single parent and that you felt you were boring.

*Jane:* Yes.

*Counsellor:* Suppose for the moment that Dave does pull out of the relationship. What would go through your mind then?

*Jane:* I'd think that everything is empty and there is no point. Life is very hard on one's own.

*Counsellor:* What would you feel about you?

*Jane:* Oh, that this is typical. I am a loser and better just accept that. It's pointless to try to make meaningful relationships. I get this sense of being unlovable somehow, you know like deep down there is something wrong with me. So I am going to be on my own. That really makes me depressed. Everything seems so empty.

In this case we see that the disappointment is linked with a number of more catastrophic thoughts about self as boring, being unlovable and destined to be alone. The counsellor listens for *key words* that may *act as markers* for underlying beliefs, e.g. boring, empty, pointless.

Sometimes one might say: 'Let's explore the worst. Let us for the moment suppose that X has happened. Now what is going through your mind?' Very often in depressed clients the worst is about being abandoned, rejected, worthless, pointless and powerless.

Sometimes if clients find it difficult to put thoughts into words a counsellor might ask a client to imagine a situation and talk about the inner picture in their minds. One person who was having difficulty expressing his thoughts about his depression in language was asked to describe a picture. After some thought he said:

> It's like I can see this party going on and I'm standing in the garden or somewhere. It's very cold, maybe snowing and very dark. I know that no matter what I do I will not be allowed in, but must stay outside just looking in and being on my own.

## Complex chains

Dryden (1989d) has recently articulated the importance of complex chains; that is, how one set of ideas and conclusions sets off another set of ideas and conclusions, or how one theme triggers another. This is a common problem in depressed clients. They may say things like 'My head is full of so many thoughts' or 'Everything is just zooming about inside.' For example, a person became angry because she thought that someone was deliberately doing something to hurt her. However, the experience of anger led to fear, with the thought, 'If I get angry I may get out of control. If I get out of control I will look silly and be humiliated.' So she believed she would not say anything, but then was resentful because of the thought, 'Why do I never stand up for myself and let others push me around. I am a weakling.' Hence thoughts about being hurt and pushed around, thoughts about looking silly, and thoughts about herself as a weakling were all tied up together. In such cases the counsellor attempts to help the person stay with one theme at a time.

Dryden (1989d) points out that if a person gets into a high state of affect it may be very difficult to get out of this cycle with cognitive restructuring. Typical is the depressed person who says, 'I understand the ideas but when I get really low I can't get out of it.' Sometimes distracting physical activity, like running or digging the garden, and at other times working on graded tasks, can be helpful. Relaxation is rarely helpful especially if this increases focus on self and rumination on thoughts. Hence distraction which involves some motor activity can be more effective. Also in these situations the counsellor identifies complex chains (or interacting themes) and teaches early identification. Here it is preventive measures that must be taken. The client learns that if they spiral down then it is difficult to get out, so they 'get in early' with coping responses.

*Specificity*
Cognitive counselling for depression follows behavioural analysis in that there is concern to be very specific about the events (antecedents) and eliciting situations. Depressed clients are often vague about things that cause their depression to increase or reduce and need to work to become more focused. When this happens it is sometimes possible to arrive at a list of specific situations that trigger negative affects, thoughts and beliefs. Specificity helps to target interventions and also to focus the client on the fact that things can become manageable and controllable.

The key issues in exploring automatic thoughts are as follows:

---

Key issues 3.2   Exploring automatic thoughts

1  The use of certain types of questions, such as when, what, why and how, help the client to clarify what is going through his/her mind.
2  These questions are aimed at facilitating guided discovery.
3  Sometimes the counsellor can use mental images and/or pictures rather than rely on spoken words.
4  At other times the counsellor can explore using the client's fantasies, such as 'Let's imagine that . . . .'
5  Counsellors may need to move into core fears in depressed clients with 'Let's assume the worst . . . .'
6  Depressed clients often have various sets of thoughts that become complex chains with interacting themes. At these times the counsellor tries to be specific by following one theme or idea at a time.
7  Clarity is helped by writing down thoughts, e.g. with the triple column technique.

---

## Rules, assumptions and attitudes

Life rules can be regarded as the instructions or beliefs that relate to happiness and avoidance of pain and unpleasantness (e.g. 'To be happy I must be loved' or 'I must be successful', and so forth). Certain rules and attitudes have been developed into the dysfunctional attitude scale (DAS) (see Blackburn and Davidson, 1990: 211–14, for a copy of this scale). Here are some typical dysfunctional attitudes, from the DAS:

4) If I do not do well all the time, people will not respect me.
11) If I can't do something well there is no point in trying.
16) I am nothing if a person I love doesn't love me.
23) I should be upset if I make a mistake.
25) To be a good, moral, worthwhile person I must always put the needs of others first.

Dysfunctional attitudes measure various domains and social themes, such as perfectionism and approval (e.g. 'People will probably think less of me if I make a mistake'; 'If a person asks for help it is a sign of weakness'). Much work has now been conducted with the dysfunctional attitude scale in depression. It has been found that depressed clients score significantly higher on the DAS than nondepressed people. However, so do many client groups and dysfunctional attitudes are not specific to depression. DAS scores correlate with neuroticism (Teasdale and Dent, 1987). It has also been found that the DAS is mood sensitive and subject to changes in mood state.

### Traps, dilemmas and snags

Ryle (1990) has explored various cognitive concepts and expressed them in a helpful framework. He has suggested repetitive themes (called traps, dilemmas and snags) in various forms of psychopathology, which are especially relevant to depression. These set up various (approach-avoidance) conflicts, increase arousal and lead to confusion.

*Traps* These are negative assumptions leading to various forms of behaviour, the consequences of which reinforce the assumptions. For example, 'I am boring to others, therefore they won't be interested in what I have to say, therefore I won't say anything – result, I behave in a boring way and people lose interest in me' (see chapter 2).

*Dilemmas* In dilemmas a person acts as though available solutions or possible roles are limited to polarized alternatives (false dichotomies). Often they are unaware that this is the case. For example, 'Either I express my feelings (but then get rejected), or I conceal them (but then feel resentful). If I love someone then I must give in to all their wishes.' In cognitive counselling this is called black–white thinking and uses the 'if then' style of thinking.

*Snags* Appropriate goals or roles are abandoned (a) on the (true or false) assumption that others would oppose them, or (b) independently of the views of others as if they were forbidden or dangerous. The depressed individual may be more or less aware that he/she acts in this way and may relate this to feelings such as guilt. In cognitive counselling we use the advantages–disadvantages approach to explore this aspect (see chapters 4 and 6). For example, 'If I get better I might be more assertive but then I might not like myself or become more like my (disliked) mother.' Snags manifest themselves in the 'yes but' styles of thinking. Many counsellors have pointed out that depressed clients often engage in 'yes but' responses.

The key issues and attributes of dysfunctional attitudes are as follows:

---

Key issues 3.3  Dysfunctional attitudes

1 Dysfunctional attitudes are often generalized 'rules for living'.
2 They are over-rigid and generalized and involve concepts like always, never, must, should, have to. Dysfunctional attitudes lack flexibility.
3 They are dysfunctional because they keep us from our goals or lead to poor role enactments (e.g. the more I have to be close to someone the more this may drive them away; or, I believe that I must never fail so I withdraw and don't try at all).
4 They can lead to various traps, snags and dilemmas.
5 In depression they tend to be focused on approval, achievement and/or control.
6 In depression they are often related to various roles (I must be caring, I must be loved, I must gain respect).
7 Dysfunctional attitudes are linked to basic self-experience (I feel bad if a rule is broken, but good if successful). The occasional positive reinforcement of them may maintain them.
8 They are linked to basic hopes in the future (e.g. If I am loved then I will be happy; if I am successful then I will be good – a somebody rather than a nobody).
9 They are often culturally reinforced (e.g. We should be individualistic and achieve, or women should be always loving and caring).

---

History

Parents

Siblings

Peers/friends

Teachers/bosses

|  | Self | Other |
|---|---|---|
| **Positive** | Able, loving, caring trusting, friendly worthy, competent attractive, good, etc. | Able, loving, caring trusting, friendly worthy, competent attractive, good, etc. |
| **Negative** | Unable, unloving incompetent, hostile neglectful, bad selfish, ugly | Unable, unloving incompetent, hostile neglectful, bad selfish, ugly |

Figure 3.1 *Development of self–other schemata serving mentalities.*

## Self–other schemata

The work on schemata is one of the most important developments in cognitive counselling in recent years. As cognitive counselling has become interested in the more long-term and complex forms of depression, the role of schemata has become paramount. Schemata relate to central and basic organizing systems for knowledge about the self and others. These are built up through life as the result of interpersonal experiences (figure 3.1).

However, there are other domains such as, 'How I think others see me' (e.g. as able, kind, etc.), and 'How I want others to see me'. Cognitive counsellors also make a distinction between conditional and unconditional self–other schemata. A conditional view is 'I am good if . . .', whereas an unconditional view is 'I am bad regardless, i.e. there is nothing I can do to make me into a good person' (Beck et al., 1990).

In uncomplicated depressive episodes it is believed that there is a switch from previous (usually) positive schemata of self and others to the activation of negative schemata (e.g. I used to feel okay about myself but now I feel a failure). This is important for counselling because it is believed that stored in long-term memory is a set of positive schemata, and working at the level of automatic thoughts and attitudes, gaining and testing hypotheses, will help to reactivate these positive schemata which do exist, but have become latent in the depression (Beck et al., 1979; Fennell, 1989; Blackburn and Davidson, 1990).

In depressions associated with personality disorder, however, positive schemata of self and others may not exist or at least may be very fragile even at the best of times (e.g. I have rarely felt okay about myself and always felt a failure). Hence, techniques to reactivate and tap into a person's premorbid level of functioning are ineffective because there is rather little (in long-term memory) to tap into. The counselling with personality disorders then becomes much more one of developing something 'anew'. This takes much longer, and requires a different focus of counselling, especially on the importance of the therapeutic relationship (Beck et al., 1990). Hence it is important to gain some idea of the person's premorbid level of functioning. However, it is erroneous to think in terms of personality disorder versus non-personality disorder. In reality these are dimensional issues and all of us have areas where our basic self–other schemata could do with a little development. Also most personality disorders show major overlaps and many clients show various aspects of them. Nevertheless, novice counsellors often attempt to use techniques designed for non-personality disordered folk with clients with personality disorders, to the disappointment and frustration of all concerned. The main issue here is one of, 'how much in the way of growth and new schemata does the person need to develop?' A number of counsellors take the view that in many cases we grow out of our psychopathologies, and the issue of maturation and new learning (rather than reactivating positive schemata) is a key issue in counselling. These developments greatly enrich the cognitive model and offer up new ways of working therapeutically.

The key issues in self–other schemata are outlined below:

---

Key issues 3.4   Self–other schemata

1   There are basic core self–other belief structures (e.g. I am. You are).
2   The counsellor needs to explore whether there has been a major shift from previous positive self–other schemata to negative schemata, or an accentuation of negative self–other schemata.

---

3 Once activated, these schemata tend to be self-perpetuating and defended against change; that is, the person distorts information to maintain them (e.g. by personalization and focusing on the negative).

4 In some clients, although their schemata are negative they are also comfortable by being familiar – what is known and predictable.

5 When a schema is activated, it tends to generate high (usually) defensive arousal and trigger defensive responses (fight/flight/avoidance etc).

6 Our basic self–other schemata often come from early life.

7 Thus they may be difficult to articulate in language but are 'experienced' as feeling states.

8 Sometimes a client feels and behaves 'as if' negative schemata are operative even though they may not be able verbally to label the schemata.

9 Typical triggers of schemata are lack of recognition or control, and actual or potential losses of valued relationships.

10 They often activate complex interacting chains of thoughts and feelings, giving the experience of 'many things rushing through one's mind' and a sense of fragmenting and falling apart.

## Conceptualization of a case

Let us now try to put these various aspects together. We can conceptualize a recent case of depression as representing an interaction of previous life history, the development of self–other schemata and basic attitudes to life, roles and basic interpersonal styles, critical incidents that lead to negative self-evaluations, and automatic thoughts (see Fennell, 1989).

*Early experiences*
Parents only seemed to pay me any attention if I was successful and achieved things. Failures led to punishment or neglect or being ignored and feeling a disappointment to them. I learned to feel disappointed in myself if I failed.

*Self–other schemata*
I can only value myself and feel in a positive relationship to others if I am succeeding. Others will only value/like me if they see I am successful and worthy.

*Basic attitudes and rules for living*
I have to show others that I am competent and try hard.
I have to achieve things to maintain my sense of self-worth.
Without success I will be ignored and not respected or attended to.
To feel good about myself I have to have others' admiring attentions.
Without success, if people got too close to me they would discover I am empty.

*Roles and social behaviour*
In relation to others I have to show how competent and successful I am.
It is more important that others praise me than I praise and value them.
If others get in my way then I withdraw or compete with them.
If others want things from me (like time in intimate relationships or having fun) that could distract me from my life goal then I must distance myself.

*Critical incidents and situations triggering depression*
Lack of recognition, admiring attention.
Failures of various kinds at college, work etc.
Entrapments (e.g. my need to earn money means I cannot pursue qualifications).
Being marginalized.

*Negative automatic thoughts*
It's my fault I am not successful.
I am not good enough. I am useless.
I will never make it. It is all too difficult.
There is no point in trying.
Others will not like or respect me.
I have no control over my life.

*Depression*

| *Symptoms* | *Social behaviour* |
|---|---|
| Loss of energy. | Withdrawal from others. |
| Increased performance anxiety. | Angry/irritable with others. |
| Strong wish to escape, hide. | Reduced positive social interaction. |

This scenario is not untypical in achievers and is often associated with alcohol problems. By conceptualizing a case in these terms it is possible to have an overview which acts as a kind of map. This helps clarity in understanding and also negotiating interventions. Thus, first one may focus interventions on the automatic thoughts. Later one may focus on dysfunctional attitudes and role behaviours. Although we have suggested the sequence of (a) obtaining the story, (b) exploring preferred scenarios and (c) moving to these preferred scenarios (Egan, 1990), it is important to recognize that if the dysfunctional attitudes, role enactments and self–other schemata (or in Kohut's, 1977, terms self object relations) are not addressed then, although the client might gain some temporary relief by reactivating his/her abilities to be successful, he/she will still remain vulnerable to future episodes. Thus, although the client's preferred scenario might be 'to be successful and gain recognition from others', the counsellor should also help the client recognize the potential dangers in these solutions. Here the counsellor might address the underlying sense of emptiness in the self, the conditional self-beliefs and so on.

## Concluding comments

Counselling depends on the enactment of a certain kind of interpersonal relationship (Dryden, 1989b). It is not a friendship (although it is conducted in a friendly way), but a collaborative endeavour with the focus on the client's internal experience and his/her social behaviour (including the social behaviour expressed in the counselling, e.g. control, avoidance etc). The qualities and skills of the counsellor, in terms of their ability to make contact with the client's internal experience, is central to counselling work. Clients who feel they are misunderstood and their internal experience unrecognized are unlikely to cooperate in counselling or reveal and work through painful experiences.

However, it is helpful for the counsellor to have some kind of understanding of the process of depression and a map for exploring and intervening. Cognitive counselling does this by helping the counsellor think about particular aspects of the client's style of interpreting, make meaning of his/her life experiences, and develop life goals and more satisfactory relational styles.

# 4

# Changing and Intervening

So far, we have explored the basic concepts of the cognitive-interpersonal model. In this chapter we will focus on the techniques for bringing about change. It is wise to remember that, while techniques are important, much research continues to show the crucial role of the counselling relationship as an agent of change (Beckham, 1990). So try not to become mesmerized by these techniques and watch out for your own automatic thoughts (see chapter 8).

## Basic philosophy for change

We have already noted that cognitive counselling is based on a philosophical approach which originated in the Stoics. These philosophers were concerned with the nature of subjective meaning – what is beauty, what is honour, what is justice? None of these questions can be answered by recourse to objective science, but rather arise from the application of various (often personal) criteria. Consequently, the Stoics were interested in the qualities that make up subjective meaning and they developed a method of enquiry to do this, called the Socratic Method of Dialogue. This dialogue was designed to reveal the underlying criteria for meaning and to expose it to refutation. It was also designed to explore the process of reasoning by which an individual comes to a certain view. Let us look at an example. A soldier (S) and a philosopher (P) have a discussion about bravery:

> S: I know what bravery is.
> P: Okay, could you tell me what you mean by bravery and maybe we could start with examples.
> S: Bravery is going to battle knowing that you will die but going anyway.
> P: Is such behaviour always bravery?
> S: Yes.
> P: Suppose that the person had no choice, that he would die via torture if he tried to leave the field. Would that be bravery?

Now, cognitive counselling revolves around the nature of the Socratic Method of Dialogue and it is important that we understand what this is. Some counsellors get this confused with debating or arguing, which it is not (at least in its counselling application). In fact, the counsellor attempts to find examples or explore homework that would help the depressed client re-evaluate his/her interpretations and beliefs, and develop new ones; that is, the dialogue is designed to help the client do psychological work and this does not involve trying to prove them wrong. It is not about positive thinking, looking on the bright side, ignoring negative or social realities. Rather, it involves exploring personal meaning and attempting to change states of mind by a gentle revelation that labels like inferiority are subjective judgements not facts; fears can be confronted and overcome; the lost relationship can be worked through and new life-style changes can be achieved. This involves enabling a person to explore and recognize that the way they reason about themselves and others is dysfunctional to the extent that they suffer greatly and do not move forward to their goals and aspirations. There is, in the Buddhist tradition, a distinction between purposeful and purposeless suffering, and many, but not all (Gut, 1989), depressions have much about them that is purposeless and are just endless spirals of despair that block exploration and growth. Thus, counselling the depression is also a journey of exploration, growth and change (Katakis, 1989).

## The process of change

The important aspect of challenging is helping depressed clients see different options, working with these options and testing things out, and this does *not* involve debating or trying to convince the person that he/she is wrong in some way. If one goes down that road one is more likely to run into resistance (Egan, 1990), or one may end up with compliance and not collaboration.

For example, suppose someone says, 'My life is completely empty.' A poor response would be 'Surely there is something positive', or 'It can't be all bad', or 'Maybe you are being overly negative because you are depressed.' A better approach is to ask, 'In what ways does your life seem particularly empty?' then, 'How would you like it to change?', and then to explore the possibilities for moving towards the alternative, preferred scenario and possible blocks.

### Collaborative empiricism

Cognitive counselling for depression is centred on collaborative empiricism (Beck et al., 1979). This means two things: first,

continually checking with the person that you have a mutual understanding and engaging the person to become involved in the
process of change, which involves helping the person plan his/her
own homework, and become actively engaged in the explorative
process rather than being reliant on the skills of the counsellor.
Second, it is an 'evidence' and 'personal theory testing' based
approach; that is, there is a focus on the evidence and the nature
of interpretation of that evidence.

Collaborative approaches require the counsellor to be sensitive to
the interpersonal style of the client (see chapter 2). The techniques
for change need to be embedded in the basic counselling qualities
and skills, and the collaborative approach outlined here. While
techniques are relatively easy to describe, *their simplicity is decep-
tive*. Counsellors who have only had the opportunity to read books
often get the idea that once a technique has been used then that
should be the end of that particular problem because the client now
knows how to be different. This is far from reality. In fact, even
the most obvious of beliefs (e.g. I am a failure) can take many
hours of work before the person gradually gets the hang of the idea
that performance and personhood (performance evaluation and
self-evaluation) need not be equated. When one reads in the books
about various alternative thoughts that clients might generate, what
is sometimes not said is that these can be the product of hours of
careful work, emotional exploration, looking at it in this way and
then that, and so on. Part of the problem here is that some
counsellors came to cognitive counselling with some cultural notion
of the Freudian view that once insight and catharsis are achieved
change is at hand. Far from it. This is often only the first step and
much work remains to be done in terms of exposure, trial-and-
error learning, developing new skills and gaining confidence in
those skills, learning, working through disappointments, finding
hidden blocks, and so forth.

Helpful procedures for challenging depressive thinking are listed
below, but these must be set within a context of a therapeutic relationship. None of these is in any sense a magical change process
– rather they represent ways of working to be conducted in the
atmosphere of 'caring interest' and an empathic relationship.
Evidence suggests eight main counselling issues which tend to be
associated with good outcome:

1 Role structuring and creating a therapeutic alliance.
2 Developing commitment for change.
3 Conducting behavioural analysis (what happens when, how,
  etc).

4 Negotiating treatment objectives (what are we trying to achieve, is there agreement on this?)
5 Executing treatment tasks and maintaining motivation.
6 Monitoring and evaluating progress.
7 Programming for generalization beyond the counselling situation (e.g. teaching antidepressant behaviour).
8 Preparing the client for the termination of treatment.

Given these preliminary comments, we are now able to explore specific kinds of intervention. In general, these fall into the main areas of: monitoring and recording; awareness training; working on specific thoughts and beliefs; behavioural approaches and role enactments; and developing positive schemata.

## Monitoring and recording

*Understanding the model*  It is important that the depressed client understands the model and its aim. You can use examples to demonstrate the links between thinking and feeling (e.g. the sound in the kitchen example in chapter 3). Clients need to understand what is going on, rather than thinking, 'Well, I guess the counsellor must know what (he/she) is doing.' The client's engagement in understanding helps to bring him/her into the counselling process.

*Understanding the issue of meaning*  It is useful to explain that meaning may be implicit rather than explicit. Meanings may need to be articulated, but may be difficult to articulate. Clients do not walk around with well-articulated attitudes and schemata in their minds. Meaning is often not coded in language so it needs to be worked with in different ways, e.g. pictures, images or re-enactments. Metaphor is another good way to help convey meaning. Hence, although one will try to put things into spoken and written language, this does not mean that the thoughts that are associated with distress occur to the person in the best spoken English.

*Self-monitoring*  This is achieved by encouraging the depressed client to become aware of, and then monitor, his/her thoughts, affects and behaviours. This alone can have therapeutic value. Various thought records can be used for this (see below). However, some depressed clients find this difficult and may tend to produce some automatic thoughts just before coming to counselling to please the counsellor. Also clients may not be very skilled, at least to begin with, in identifying their thoughts. Sometimes diary keeping is a useful procedure here also. The client makes a record of events, thoughts, feelings and actions at the end of the day. Diaries can then be the source for joint exploration. However, it is usually more effective to try to encourage clients to be aware of their thoughts as they actually happen (Safran and Segal, 1990) and especially in the counselling session. Hence the issue of monitoring is a key aspect of counselling.

*Degree of belief*   It is helpful to explore with the depressed client the degree or extent to which they believe something is true. This can be given a percentage rating. As we shall discuss later, beliefs are not always all or nothing and in counselling depressed people one may see changes in the degree of a belief rather than its absolute removal. Sometimes even a 10 per cent change is a major change.

*Writing down*   Clients often find it helpful to write things down. In the early stages the counsellor and client may do this together. Later clients do it for themselves. One simple method is with the use of two columns. In one column the depressing thoughts are written, and in the other various alternative and challenging thoughts. This is called the double column technique.

| *Depressing thoughts* | *Alternative/coping thoughts* |
|---|---|
| I will never be better | 1 This idea makes me feel worse and I may be underselling myself. |
| | 2 I can work on small steps towards understanding my depression and overcoming it. |
| | 3 I haven't always been depressed so I have shown myself I am capable of coping. |
| | 4 Because things are difficult right now doesn't mean they will always be difficult. |
| Degree of belief: 75% | Degree of belief: 50% |

As we work on the depression, the degree of belief in 'I will never be better' slowly reduces and this is indicative of improvement.

*Agenda setting* Cognitive counselling tries to be clear about agendas. Hence at the beginning of each session it is often helpful to form an agenda for the session. This involves monitoring thoughts and feelings about the previous session, checking mood, checking on homework, and deciding the crucial areas to be covered in the session to come. However, the counsellor needs to be careful since some clients can hold back issues until well into a session. So at all times the counsellor remains flexible. For example, a client's mother had died between sessions but the counsellor had focused on a homework that had gone badly and spent most of the session exploring this. Also, if one is too rigid the client may rely on the counsellor and not bring his/her own material.

## Awareness training

The next set of techniques involves helping the depressed client gain increased awareness of the role of their beliefs and personal meanings in their depression.

*Role play* Role play is a powerful technique for eliciting various forms of meaning and is a useful way of eliciting affect and demonstrating the power of cognitions in the counselling situation. There are a number of ways this can be done. For example, a person who is frightened of behaving assertively may be asked to role play an assertive sequence of behaviour. The counsellor then explores the beliefs about this (e.g. I am being unkind, other people will think I am being selfish and I must maintain other people's approval; or, I will be embarrassed and go blank). Other forms of role play can involve the re-enactment of previous painful events, e.g. arguments. Again, the counsellor can check the meanings that the person constructs about these episodes. Subsequently, they can practice alternative behaviours and cognitive responses. Clients are encouraged to try out their new skills and cognitions in real-life situations.

As a rule of thumb, role play works best when the client and counsellor have developed a good working alliance. Without this the client may not really get into the role play but just mimic it, and not really be in touch with the powerful emotions that need to be understood and worked with.

*The two chairs* Another technique for increasing awareness of the 'power of the internal (often negative-hostile) self-dialogue' and its emotive effects is the two chairs technique (Greenberg, 1979; Greenberg and Safran, 1987; Greenberg et al., 1990; Safran and

Segal, 1990). In this situation the counsellor elicits the negative dialogue in the form of an inference chain (e.g. I failed to get the job, nobody will respect me, I'm a complete bum). This is written on a card and placed in one chair. The client is then invited to sit in this chair and read the card to the chair opposite (e.g. saying 'You didn't get the job, nobody will respect you, you are a complete bum'). When a certain level of affect has been put in to this, the client changes back and sits in the chair at which they directed the attack, and they are asked to explore their feelings about this attack being levelled against them. Often this involves sadness, anger, helplessness etc.

In this way the client gains deeper and more emotional insight into the power of their internal thoughts about themselves. One can also ask things like, 'Did that voice of attack remind you of anyone?' Sometimes this may turn out to be a parental figure. This can have the effect of bringing in a high level of affect and the counsellor is sensitive to allow this to emerge and work gently with it rather than rush in with cognitive restructuring. Later, the client can be encouraged to 'fight back' to the negative dialogue, e.g. 'Just because I didn't get the job doesn't make me a bum; you keep running me down and your attacks are the source of my problem; how about a bit of support right now?' At these times it is useful to enable the person to say what they would like to. If a parental figure has been identified as the source of the negative self-dialogue, then they may wish to say things like 'Why were you always running me down? Why didn't you help and support me?' Again, these exchanges can get quite emotional and powerful so it is useful to gain some experience and training before trying out this approach. I include it here to show how it can be used to increase awareness, make contact with affect, and help the client to dispute internal self-downing.

*Drawing out recursive feedback*    Cognitive counsellors often like to make a diagram of their summaries with a client to give a visual overview. This is especially helpful to show positive recursive feedback, which can be drawn as a circle (figure 4.1). For example, 'I feel depressed – when depressed I can't do anything – when I can't do anything I feel useless – when I feel useless I get more depressed – when I get more depressed I do less' etc.

The positive feedback nature or the spirals of these patterns can be demonstrated for cognitions and behaviours. Discussion can centre on where best to intervene and help make predictions; for example, 'If you could stop putting yourself down when you feel unable to do things would this be helpful? What would be the

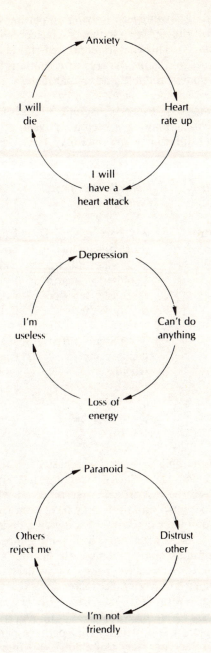

**Figure 4.1** *Positive recursive feedback in diagrammatic form.*

advantages and disadvantages of giving up putting yourself down?'
Also, one can write out the sequence conceptualising a case (as
shown in chapter 3). This enables depressed clients to gain an overview of the issues and helps the role of cognitions in depression to
become more understandable and manageable.

*Working with the past*   It can be useful for clients to recognize that
their ways of coping may have been adaptive at one time, and are
not evidence of inferiority or stupidity. Here we can use three
columns.

| Current belief | Contributing past experiences | Alternatives |
|---|---|---|
| I have no control over my life | 1 My parents said I must always do as I was told.<br>2 I had to change schools often due to my father's job.<br>3 My parents often disliked my friends. | 1 I am an adult now and can choose.<br>2 I can stay where I am now if I wish.<br>3 My choice of friends depends on my feelings and preferences. |
| Degree of belief: 80% | Degree of belief: 100% | Degree of belief: 45% |

In the above example, it is not just a case of writing things down
but using the columns to clarify meanings and experiences, such
that (in this case) the person gains insight as to why it seems 'as
if' they have no control (and this may have been true at one time)
but they can now make changes. This involves giving up trying to
please parents or fit in with others and gaining more confidence in
one's own decisions and preferences. In the above case, as
counselling progressed, we saw changes in the degree of belief, with
column 1 reducing and column 3 increasing. This indicates again
that counselling is a process and rarely produces sudden change.

Depressed clients who have problems with guilt about not caring
enough can explore the possibility that perhaps parents used guilt
to control them and that they can change this internal evaluation
now. Thus the writing down is for the clarification it brings, and
acts as a focus for discussion. In the alternatives column it is

important that clients genuinely recognize the thoughts and ideas as alternatives and not as another form of instruction (this time coming from the counsellor, i.e. I believe(d) that, but really I ought to believe this).

*Nonverbal behaviour* To increase awareness it is often useful to be attentive to the depressed client's nonverbal behaviour (Safran and Segal, 1990), the clenched hand or jaw or the averted eyes. The counsellor can draw attention to this, e.g. 'I noted, while you were taking about your girl friend, that your jaw seemed clenched and tight. Could you focus on your jaw and explore what was going through your mind?' or 'What is your jaw saying?' Sometimes clients are not aware of these nonverbal changes. Directing their attention to them is helpful and illuminating.

*Fantasies* These serve various functions. Fantasy can be our inspiration, a way of escaping reality, or our projections into the future. For example, a depressed client with a difficult life situation would often fantasize that someone would come and rescue her, rather than her changing her situation (which she felt powerless to do). Under stress she would always have in the back of her mind, 'Never mind one day someone will come.' As the years passed and things got worse, this fantasy could no longer sustain her. In another case, whenever a client had an argument she would simply switch off and fantasize being alone. In this way she never engaged in conflict but nevertheless became unhappy with the idea, 'It's no good I shall have to live alone, relationships are just too difficult.' She would then spend many hours planning how to cope alone. Sometimes fantasies can even be of death. Depressive fantasies often contain an 'if only' element.

It is not always the case that clients will tell you of their repetitive fantasies (sometimes due to shame and sometimes due to the feeling these are part of the deepest, inner self), and therefore one has to ask for them (e.g. 'What are your main fantasies or day dreams? When you find yourself wandering off into your inner thoughts, what kind of thoughts and images do you have?').

Some clients may have fantasies about the counsellor and this can also be explored. A client may feel that the counsellor might have sexual desires for them, or they may have sexual desire for the counsellor, or that the counsellor is secretly thinking they are a hopeless case. These transference ideas and fantasies can be very disruptive to the collaborative relationship if not addressed (Watkins, 1989a), but the counsellor needs to work sensitively so as not to act in a rejecting way while maintaining clear boundaries.

*The journal* This is similar to diary keeping but here the counsellor encourages the client to write a diary of their thoughts as they are going through counselling. With some clients it is helpful to suggest they write a diary of why they think they have become depressed, to write a mini autobiography and to note repetitive themes. This does not suit all clients but some really enjoy it and find the act of writing about themselves gives them a new insight and awareness. The client can write anything he/she likes here from past memories to current reflections on counselling. One client did this and then while on a trip threw her journal out of the train window in a symbolic gesture to mark a new beginning.

The key issues in awareness training and self-monitoring are given below.

---

Key issues 4.1  Awareness training and self-monitoring

1 As part of change the client needs to become more aware of his/her internal meaning-making, thoughts, beliefs and schemata.
2 Awareness training can take various forms such as re-enactments, a focus on images, fantasies, nonverbal behaviour and two chairs.
3 Awareness is focused on the links between internal meaning and affective state.
4 Once these meanings and cognitive styles are identified, they are subjected to progressive clarification and exposure (e.g. by writing the thoughts down).
5 Clients can learn how to monitor more closely their internal life and in this way, with increased awareness, make it subject to change.

---

## Targeting specific thoughts and beliefs

In cognitive counselling with depressed clients there are often specific cognitions and beliefs that one wishes to target for change.

*Looking at the evidence* Evidence testing is a key element of cognitive counselling, but what constitutes evidence? What the counsellor thinks is evidence the client may not, or the client may have unarticulated ways of disqualifying it – this needs checking. Many of the interventions below are about checking and testing evidence.

*Is there enough information?* Sometimes depressed clients focus on very small aspects of the situation and it is useful to encourage a wider exploration. For example, 'Jenny seemed off with me last night. I am sure that she is losing interest in me.' The counsellor can then explore how Jenny behaved when she met the client last night. Did Jenny give any information about why she was quiet? Exploring the situation may reveal information like, 'Well, actually Jenny is worried about losing her job.' This can then lead to looking at alternatives, e.g. Jenny was off because she felt down and worried and she tends to withdraw when she is worried.

*Looking at, or for, alternatives* Looking for alternatives is an important aspect of considering evidence. Sometimes depressed clients are convinced that there is only one way to view things. Here one teaches the client to consider thoughts as theories or hypotheses, and the more theories and hypotheses one has the better. This is similar to Kelly's (1955) view of teaching people how to treat themselves as scientists. So one explores the generation of alternative ideas/views, e.g. 'Can you think of any other reasons why this may have happened?' or 'Can you think of any other reasons why Jenny was off with you last night?'

*Thinking in blends, shades or dimensionally* A very common difficulty in depression is dichotomous thinking or thinking in black and white. In analytic theory this is called 'splitting'. There are two aspects here. Basic black–white thinking and coping with ambivalence.

For basic black–white thinking there are various challenges. One is to draw a straight line with a bipolar construct. For example, suppose a client says, 'My performance was a complete failure.' The counsellor may draw a line like this:

| | |
|---|---|
| Failure ——————————— | Success |
| Bad | Good |
| Terrible | Wonderful |

The client then places an X on the line to show the degree of success/failure he/she thinks applies to them. Often this is put close to the end. The counsellor then discusses various other behaviours that might rate as greater failures to illuminate how the person's construct is rather narrow. One can talk in terms of focusing on the achievements or the failures, the glass that is half-full or half-empty. Again the technique is only an aid to help the client understand the nature of their absolutistic thinking, and much discussion is also involved.

Dealing with ambivalence and helping clients recognize that we often have shades or blends of feeling in the same situation can be more difficult depending on the case. These can present as dilemmas (Ryle, 1990), e.g. 'If I love someone then I should never feel angry or want to leave them. If someone loves me they should never want to leave me.' Here the counsellor may use information from everyday life, e.g. quoting the song, 'You always hurt the one you love.' However, making clear that ambivalence is part of life can take time for the client to accept since in some cases there is a need for certainty.

In feminist approaches, derived from Jung's ideas, there is concern with flow and rhythm between different possibilities. That is, we cannot parcel up life into neat boxes and rank things in some kind of order of inferior–superior, accept–reject. Thus internal life needs to be understood as part of a whole rather than segregated into good and bad. In everything there can be helpful or unhelpful elements. Jung's concept was that everything casts a shadow. Some clients take to this kind of discussion and gain deeper insights into black–white thinking.

*Distinguishing self-rating from behavioural rating*   This is a very common problem in depression and is often reinforced culturally. Basically, if my performance is imperfect then 'I' (as a person) am a failure (Ellis, 1977a,b). Here one teaches the damage of self-rating, focusing on the internal dialogue (e.g. with the friend technique [see below] or the two chairs). Also use the little *i* and big *I* to show how clients may be making global generalizations from single events. Sometimes we call this the IT–ME confusion. I only accept ME if I do IT well. IT–ME confusions often lie behind ideas of worth(lessness) and also self-labelling. Hence we try to teach self-understanding and acceptance, and again much discussion can be given over to this issue.

IT–ME confusions are perhaps part of Western culture; they are very common and the counsellor should be clear in his/her own mind about this. As Fennell (1989: 205) says, this is a case of physician heal thy self. In training counsellors I have found that many find this a basic problem, 'But surely your worth is dependent on how competent you are!' The counsellors who have this basic belief may have problems in helping their clients change it.

*Mourning the lost chance or ideal*   It is important when challenging IT–ME confusions to recognize that there may be a secret fantasy about what success would bring (e.g. 'If I could get my performance perfect then I would be successful. Only if I am successful will I be loved and respected'). This is a competitive and narcissistic theme. As argued elsewhere, sometimes clients find it difficult to come to terms with ordinary human failings because they wish to be superior to others (Gilbert, 1989). By being superior they think they will fulfil basic human needs for love, respect, admiration etc. Hence it often happens that overcoming resistance to changing IT–ME thinking may involve the opportunity to mourn the lost ideal possibility (see chapter 6). The advantages–disadvantages (see below) can be a useful technique to help explore this aspect. Hence IT–ME confusions can also involve a lot of idealizing and hope. The client will be less likely to shift on these if the underlying ideals are not addressed (see chapter 7).

*Reattribution training* In depression there can be much personalization for bad outcomes. 'It's my fault that Fred/Sally left me.' Simple interventions can involve looking at the evidence or the friend technique (see below). However, again there can be complications. For example, a depressed client may say 'If I blame them then I would be in a rage and that makes me feel bad about me.' Hence self-blame can have a protective function (we shall have more to say about assertiveness and anger in chapter 6). Indeed, the way self-blame stops one expressing anger at others can be explored in many ways (e.g. as defensive exclusion: as a child the client has learnt not to be critical of others and therefore ignores their bad behaviour towards them; Bowlby, 1980). So when self-blame arises it is always useful to keep in mind whether this is concerned with interpersonal events or not, the former being more complex, but again the advantages–disadvantages approach can be used to explore the issue of 'not taking the blame'.

The other distinction to be aware of is attribution for causes and attributions for changes or solutions:

1 It is not my fault I am depressed and there is nothing I can do to change.
2 It is my fault I am depressed and there is nothing I can do to change.
3 It is not my fault I am depressed but I can take steps to overcome depression.
4 It is my fault I am depressed and I can take steps to change.

Generally speaking, it is the third of these that the counsellor fosters. The causes of depression, and vulnerability to it, can arise from many sources, e.g. post-viral infections, hostile marriages, poor early experiences, and so forth. Getting caught up in self-blaming for causing depression is not helpful. Thus the counsellor tends to endorse a multi-factor causal model (Gilbert, 1992). Nevertheless, helping clients recognize that by putting themselves down they may maintain and worsen their depression is not taken as evidence of personal blame for depression. Dryden (1989a) points out that helping clients take responsibility for their cognitions is a central part of the counselling endeavour. The match between client and counsellor attribution for depression can be a source of difficulty that interferes with therapeutic work (for an illuminating discussion see Jack and Williams, 1991).

The other distinction that can be made in attributions, which is similar to the IT–ME confusion, is the distinction between blaming one's character and blaming one's behaviour. Generally, character (personal attributes and qualities) self-blame is more depressogenic that behavioural self-blame (Janoff-Bulman and Hecker, 1988). For example, Janoff-Bulman found that, in women who had been raped, character self-blame (it was something about me that invited it) was more commonly associated with depression than behavioural self-blame (it was something I did like walk in the wrong part of town). Dryden (1989a) suggests that there are three levels of self-blame: blaming self, blaming traits and blaming behaviour. These vary in terms of the global qualities of self-blame.

*Attitudes to feelings*    Sometimes in depression there is much resentment, envy and anger under the surface (Gilbert, 1992) but the person has difficulty in coping with these feelings because they see it as evidence of a bad self. This is Freud's concept of anger turned inward, but in cognitive counselling it is an attitudinal problem. Some feel that they do not have the right to be angry, while others feel that anger makes them unlovable, thus anger cues an internal attack and the client takes a defensive position to it. The counsellor helps the client accept his/her resentment and to recognize that nine times out of ten this relates to painful disappointment. In many cases I have found a cycle of disappointment cuing anger, anger cuing bad self-experience, and bad self-experiences cuing fears of abandonment and loss. This goes around in the person's mind leading to much confusion and distress. An empathic counsellor always has an ear open for disappointment, whether this be of the ideal, the hope or whatever, and allows the grief and anger to be explored.

*Identifying the shoulds, musts and oughts*    There are many forms of must that can emerge: I *have* to be loved, I *must* be perfect etc. The main concern here is to change a must, ought or should into an I'd like/prefer to. Hence it is changing commands or demands into preferences. One can engage the depressed client in discussion of their 'life's rule book' or our 'personal contracts with life', pointing out that musts lead to certain feelings of compulsion and lack of freedom. Or one can simply ask, 'Why do you think you must be loved?' and in this way elicit an underlying belief 'Without love I'm worthless.' Hence the worthless idea leads to the compulsion to be loved. Thus oughts, shoulds and musts are often driven by some underlying self-evaluative concept. However, in this kind of situation, it is important that the counsellor does not convey the view that there is something unacceptable in the strong desire to have a loving relationship, far from it. Rather the focus is on the sense of worthlessness not the desire. Indeed, counselling may involve helping the person acquire skills that make it more likely they can form intimate and meaningful relationships – that may be a counselling goal!

Also, the idea that life would be meaningless without success or love can be an issue. Here again one does not suggest that the goal is undesirable, rather focus is on the global evaluations and the dismissal of other sources of positive rewards. In such cases mourning may be involved as counselling unfolds, especially if these desires are highly idealized (see chapter 6).

The counsellor should also use his/her empathy to recognize when a client is using the words of should, ought or must in a relative way or in an absolutistic way. We often use should and ought words in normal, everyday language but this does not mean we see them as absolute musts. Thus clients can be asked to rate the degree of belief in their musts and shoulds.

*Flash cards*   Depressed clients can forget what has happened in the counselling session. Therefore it is helpful for them to have prompts. This can be done with the use of flash cards. This is a blank card about the size of a postcard. On one side of the card the client works out, with the counsellor, his/her thoughts, e.g. 'I am never able to do as good a job as I'd like. I always seem to fail. I am a really useless person. What's the point of trying.' Rather than having to write out these thoughts for themselves they can put a tick on the card as a thought happens. On the back, the counsellor and client work out some challenges that the client feels are helpful. For example, 'These are pretty unkind things to be saying to myself when I'm feeling down; I would not speak to a friend like this; I don't *have* to do everything perfectly; Just because my mother called me these things doesn't make it true; I can take it in stages and learn to focus on what I can do; I can define a half-full glass as half-empty or half-full', and so forth.

Different clients find different forms of challenge helpful. For one client an appeal to reason is helpful, for another the appeal to self-nurturing. Sometimes clients say 'When I looked on the back of my card I heard your voice and that was helpful.' This helps the internalization of positive self-statements and cues memory. Gradually clients learn to challenge for themselves automatically.

*The friend technique*  The friend technique involves helping the depressed client change his/her perspective on him/herself by considering interactions with a friend. One can use questions like 'Would you say this to a friend?' If you elicit a hostile internal dialogue (e.g. I failed to get the job, nobody will respect me, I'm a complete bum) then say, 'Imagine a friend sitting in this chair. She/he has told you of the same event you have told me. Can you say to her/him what you say to yourself?' Sometimes it is useful to encourage the person to speak out loud their inner dialogues but directed at a friend (e.g. to friend: 'Well, you didn't get the job, therefore nobody will respect you and you are a complete bum'). Try to help the person generate affect and to predict the impact of this attack on the friend; e.g. 'How do you think your friend would feel if you said this to them?' The key here is to help the client recognize the damage of internal put-downs – or the internal hostile relationship (see Gilbert, 1989). The second issue is to facilitate a more nurturing self-dialogue when things are not going well. Thus the focus is on identifying the 'internal bully', as I often call it, and changing this to an internal helper.

*Role reversal*  Helping the client think about how others might interpret events can be useful. Thus one can ask 'How do you think others might respond to this? What accounts for the difference?' Helping the client see things from the other person's perspective helps to move the cognitive focus away from the self. Another form of role reversal helps the client to challenge their beliefs, through being encouraged to help someone else who has the same beliefs as themselves. For example, suppose a client says 'I will never be able to succeed. I will never find the kind of relationship I need. My life is pointless and worthless.' The counsellor might say 'How might you help someone else who seemed trapped in this way of seeing things?' If the client attempts to do this, and is able to come up with alternative ways of thinking and looking at the problem, the counsellor may play devil's advocate and say 'But suppose this person said, I have tried all those things and they don't work, how would you respond to them?' In this way the counsellor avoids pitting him/herself against the client and through role reversal has encouraged the client to explore alternatives to their own negative thinking by helping someone else. The counsellor might continue this with questions like 'What do you think would stop this other person from acting on your ideas?' This enables a dialogue that helps the person to change their perspective.

*Advantages and disadvantages* This is an approach that has many uses and is used in many different therapies. It helps to show up dilemmas and it also gives clients a clear insight into what may be blocking them from change. Write out two columns headed Advantages and Disadvantages (or Gains and Losses), then list the ideas in each.

### Giving up blaming myself

| Advantages | Disadvantages |
|---|---|
| Would feel better | Might become more angry |
| Would take more risks | Might become aggressive like mother (the not nice me) |
| Would not feel so inferior | Might never see my faults |
| Would stop hurting myself | Others might not like me |
| | Might become like mother |

It is not uncommon to find that one of the disadvantages of changing is that the person sees themselves as becoming more like a disliked other. For example, in this case, the client's mother rarely blamed herself but mostly blamed the children. The client worried that by not blaming herself she might become like her (disliked) mother. Thus work focused on the type of blame (e.g. self, trait or behavioural) and helping her distinguish between blaming and responsibility. We shall explore what to do about this kind of issue more fully in chapter 6. For the moment let us explore another example.

### Giving up perfectionism

| Advantages | Disadvantages |
|---|---|
| Could relax | Might become slapdash |
| Feel less pressured | Might make mistakes |
| Could spend more time with my family | Might miss opportunities to get on |
| | Might become no better than others |
| | Would lose self-respect |

In the above case the client was sure that in becoming less of a perfectionist he would loss his self-respect. Thus, although he was quite happy 'supposedly' to work on his perfectionism in fact he was not able to until it had become clear to him the potential costs as he saw them.

There are many costs to change and the fear of change can be an important focus for counselling, e.g. 'I might be abandoned. I might not like myself. God might not like me. I might become like others whom I dislike', and so forth. Although clients can agree goals in the counselling session, it is always worth running through the potential gains and losses to highlight possible losses. No client will change if somehow they sense that changing will make them worse.

Other typical losses are: 'If I give up my anger it is condoning what others have done to me, or it is saying it does matter, or I will feel powerless. If I give up putting others first and become more focused on my needs then I will become selfish and unlovable. If I give up black–white thinking then I can never be certain, and that's dangerous', and so forth. A common disadvantage in revealing a secret, like a history of abuse, an abortion, sexual or other behaviour, is 'If I tell you then you will dislike me and won't want to help me.' The approach can be more complicated by exploring long- and short-term advantages and disadvantages.

By writing these down the client is able to be clear about the dilemmas and hold them in one frame, as it were, and then there can be a new agreement to work on not just the goal but the fears of reaching the goal. Sometimes whole sessions can be given over to this one form of intervention (see chapter 6).

*Other people's gains*  In some cases of depression it is useful to consider the possibility of what others might gain from the client's depression. In various forms of family counselling it has been noticed that as a family member's depression reduces, other problems surface. A colleague, Dr E. MacAdam, gave the example of an adolescent girl whose mother could not decide about making a long-term commitment to a new male friend. While the daughter was depressed the mother was able to avoid the problem. In the counselling the adolescent was offered the idea that her depression protected her mother from having to make a difficult decision. It had a remarkable effect by reframing the problem as protection of mother.

Hence one can speculate on issues such as 'I wonder what your spouse/family gains by your being depressed and clinging onto them.' At first a client may be perplexed by such a question, but it can 'get them thinking'. This kind of question is in part aimed to illuminate the power issues that may be involved in depression, but also to help a client see a depression in a new light; that is, paradoxically, a depressed position can actually be protective of the self or of someone else. For example, if the patient were not depressed they might leave a relationship. There is now growing evidence that depression acts to inhibit assertive behaviour and this can have the effect of maintaining the power of others (see Gilbert, 1992). Thus one can look at the advantages–disadvantages of depression to self and others.

*Additional areas and challenges*  The above are the most common forms of challenge but here are some additional areas that you may wish to discuss with clients:

1 Are they misunderstanding the nature of causes? Most events are multi-causal.
2 Are they confusing a thought or idea with fact?
3 Are they assuming that every situation is/will be the same?
4 How would they look at this if they were not depressed?
5 Are they confusing a high probability with a low probability?
6 Are they being honest with themselves?
7 Are they asking questions that have no answers?
8 How would they feel about this (event) in a month or a year?

The above offer a detailed overview of the kinds of intervention that are possible with depressed clients. The key issues in targeting specific cognitions are as follows:

---

Key issues 4.2  Targeting specific cognitions

1 The main focus is on the client's internal cognitions, inter-pretations and beliefs. Especially important in depression is the client's cognitions about him/herself, e.g. self-downing and blaming.
2 The counsellor aims to increase the client's awareness of these and their contribution to depression. Various techni-ques can be used to do this.
3 The counsellor and client try to identify typical forms of cognitive style or distortion (e.g. personalization, disqualify-ing the positive, black–white thinking).
4 Insight is important but it is not the main goal of the approach. Cognitions are treated as hypotheses and theories not facts.

5 The counsellor and client work together to decide what is evidence; is an alternative reasonable rather than just pulled out of the hat?
6 The counsellor and client recognize both the advantages and the fears/disadvantages of change.
7 There is clear discussion about IT–ME confusions and self-labelling.

## Working with schemata

There is much overlap between working on specific thoughts and behaviours and looking at schemata since these cannot be neatly separated out.

*Identify main schemata*   These may be for approval or achievement. Try to crystallize this in the counselling discussion. One may wish to refer to it as 'your/my approval schemata'. Explore how (say) approval schemata (e.g. I am unlovable) becomes easily triggered in various situations (e.g. at times of conflict or in social situations) and generates strong feelings.

*Schemata lead to roles*   Explore how certain kinds of schemata lead to certain kinds of interpersonal behaviour which may be overplayed or avoided. For example, a schemata of 'I am unlovable' may lead to the avoidance of conflict and/or an overly submissive and compliant style.

*Schemata and affect*   Help the client recognize that schemata can be part of what we feel at the core/centre of ourselves (Guidano and Liotti, 1983). Therefore, if these are aroused or threatened, they will generate high arousal and strong feelings. Hence clients may need much work and repetition in order to change. When there is strong affect, help the client recognize this may be schemata driven.

*Awareness of developmental abilities*   Some clients are not capable of abstract thinking but are still at a stage of more concrete thinking (Rosen, 1989). A counsellor needs to be aware of the cognitive and conceptual abilities of the client. Sometimes one is helping this maturation process. Consequently, try to engage in interventions that a client will understand.

## Behavioural approaches

*Homework* Teaching the value of homework is an important part of the cognitive approach, although clients vary as to the ease in which they engage in it. Homework is an essential part of cognitive counselling, not only for gathering evidence but also for beginning to develop new repertoires, skills and expectancies. It is useful to encourage the client to suggest their own homework, e.g. 'How do you think you could practice overcoming this problem?', and/or 'Given what we have been speaking about, what do you think you need (to do) to get over/help (with) this problem?'

In planning homework with depressed clients there are some useful mottoes:

1 Challenging but not overwhelming. In the same way you learn to drive, you would not go onto a motorway the first time out (i.e. homework needs to be realistic and approached as graded tasks, see also Dryden, 1985).
2 Getting better rather than feeling better. Here you can make the point that engaging fears or doubts and challenging negative cognitions may result, at first, in feeling worse. However, one can learn how to cope better and identify what the cognitions and problems are that contribute to feeling worse. Try to engage the person in their own training and encourage them to generate homework ideas. Progress should be in steps. Ask questions like 'How could you test this idea?'
3 A very common issue is the fear of getting better. Thus homework can be sabotaged. It maybe useful to use the advantages–disadvantages technique to get at this (see above). In cases of depression this issue can take most of the work.
4 Disqualifying achievements. Typical here are the ideas that 'Anyone could do that. Compared to what I used to do it is so simple.' Help clients to imagine that if they have fallen in to a deep hole it helps to have a ladder that they walk up rung by rung rather than to jump to the top. Thus the image is on 'moving forward' rather than unrealistic comparisons.

If clients say that the homework or behavioural work makes them feel worse the skilled counsellor is able to use this to advantage; e.g. 'Well, this is helpful because we can look more closely at what is going on', or 'Well, this is helpful since it shows that you are really engaging in the problem.' The counsellor should be cautious of falling into the trap of expecting the client to feel better with homework and becoming disheartened when the client says they feel worse. The more the counsellor allows the client to feel worse from homework and to use this experience constructively the easier it is for the client not to fear bringing negative information to the counselling. We want to avoid the client thinking outside counselling, 'Well, I didn't like to tell my counsellor this because he is trying so hard and it would upset him.' Also the counsellor should avoid setting him/herself up in the position of trying to get the client better. This usually leads to exhausted counsellors and problems in counselling. The process is collaboration, with agreement on the purpose of the therapeutic endeavour.

*Long- and short-term goals for change* Here the counsellor helps the client to select short-term, obtainable changes or tasks rather than be over optimistic and likely to fail. Clients are often poor at generating steps to change and may disqualify small steps (e.g. disqualifying the positive). It is also quite useful to check out the fantasies of getting/being better. Sometimes these can be quite unrealistic and over-idealized. The client may have held a belief that one day he/she would be magically better and never be unhappy or frustrated again. The slow progress of getting better, and dealing with the frustration of two steps forward and one back, all need to be worked through.

*Image substitution* In cases where anxiety is high it is useful to have clear insight into the images and fantasy. Then you can develop alternative images and fantasies with clients that they can practice in the feared situation. For example, one depressed client who was afraid of the dark had an image of being attacked but imagined herself as helpless. This had come from her early life when her mother was very physically aggressive and where passivity was the only way to reduce the attacks. Hence we taught her to practice imagining fighting back. She had never thought of this possibility but it proved a very helpful intervention in her case, especially when she had seen the connection between her passivity images and problems in her childhood. It is actually quite difficult *not* to think of something, hence advising clients not to think about their automatic thoughts does not usually work. It is better to find an alternative thought.

*Social skills training* Some depressed clients have difficulties in certain interpersonal skills, e.g. assertiveness (Argyle, 1984; Arrindell et al., 1988). In these cases instruction and behavioural practice may be helpful. One can give reading material (e.g. Dickson, 1982) or arrange for time to attend assertiveness training classes. Same-sex groups can be especially helpful. This can often be better than trying to do it all in individual counselling. In a group the client will have an opportunity to practise with others, share experiences and so forth. Here the counsellor is trying to enlarge the client's opportunities for new learning. However, skills sometimes do not generalize outside of the counselling situation. Various negative thoughts may inhibit this. Hence some clients are skilled but inhibited.

*New role enactments*   Related to social skills is the identification of how a person would like to behave socially. This can be to act assertively or more caringly. In these situations one may talk about the role, the skills that are necessary and the blocks to their enactment. For example, a depressed man wanted to show more affection to his children but felt embarrassed to do so. He was worried about being seen as sissy and his actions being misunderstood as sexual. Simple discussion of this issue and some normalization, sharing of the fears and information on the role of physical touch, was helpful. In another case, a depressed woman wanted to show more affection to her children but often felt she did this out of guilt not genuine concern. Also, after an argument she found it difficult to reconcile with them, without feeling she was giving in. However, she wanted to repair the relationships between them. So we talked about the guilt, based on her thoughts that she was not good enough, and about the value of reconciling behaviours. I used examples from chimpanzees to show the importance of reconciliation. She thought that if she instigated reconciliation she was saying she was in the wrong and was admitting defeat. Via cognitive restructuring and behavioural training she was able to make changes.

*How do clients learn?*   Some depressed clients find reading material very helpful in bringing out core dilemmas and helping to overcome negative social comparisons. Others do not. The counsellor should be aware of a range of reading material that they can recommend to their clients as appropriate.

*Anxiety reduction*   If anxiety is prominent in depression (which clinical experience and research shows it often is) then many of the behavioural techniques for anxiety control can be helpful (e.g. relaxation and desensitization, breathing control). However, some depressed clients do not find relaxation classes helpful. This is because, in depression, the client can be highly focused on internal negative ruminations and thoughts. It is often more helpful to use various forms of distraction activity that require their attention to be outwardly directed. In other words, work with what is helpful to the individual.

*Scheduling activities*　Some clients find it very difficult to carry out certain tasks because their ability to plan ahead has been affected by the depression. Scheduling activities can be taught in the counselling and worked out in a collaborative way. One client suffered from loneliness and therefore we scheduled that he should visit friends on as many evenings as possible. Activity planning can also be helpful but again while some clients take to this easily and find it helpful, others do not. So work with the individual and try not to 'force' techniques on clients because the books say so.

The main features of behavioural interventions are as follows:

---

Key issues 4.3　Behavioural interventions

1 Cognitive changes need to be translated into changes in behaviour.
2 Behavioural change and experimentation produce opportunities to gain further information and to observe blocks to change.
3 Behavioural interventions are also designed to gain new insights and practice new skills.
4 Behavioural interventions must be realistic and agreed.
5 Often the behaviour at issue is social, thus change involves new interpersonal enactments and roles.
6 Much of counselling can be understood as a process of exposure to feared internal and external experiences and situations, involving not only insight but desensitization to what is feared (e.g. assertiveness).

---

**Developing positive schemata**

A central issue in cognitive counselling has concerned the degree to which one works against negative schemata and attitudes, and/or promotes positive schemata and attitudes. Now, of course, in reality one does both and these are in no way mutually exclusive endeavours. Nevertheless, it is easy to gain the impression that cognitive counselling is about disputing the negative and dysfunctional. However, many aspects above are concerned with enabling the development of (sometimes new) skills and schemata, and in this sense there is a degree of growth and health promotion.

In some cases the therapeutic relationship can be the most

important source of developing new positive schemata of trust acceptance and self-esteem. By empathy and listening, one enables the client to experience a helpful and accepting relationship. In this way the client internalizes greater self-acceptance via the acceptance and understanding of the counsellor. Kohut (1977) has stressed the importance of mirroring the client and allowing a certain idealization. In evolutionary theory the client experiences the counsellor as someone who is prepared to invest resources in them, such as time, care, energy, skill and efforts to understand and recognize (Gilbert, 1992), and this in itself can be internalized as an important source of self-esteem (Gilbert, 1989, 1992). The point is that we should not underestimate the relationship as a major source for the development of positive self-schemata. Hence it is useful to be attentive to various factors that may reduce the client's ability to internalize the experience of this positive relationship. Experiences such as strong envy of the counsellor or unresolved doubts about the acceptability of the client in the eyes of the counsellor (e.g. shame) can significantly block the development of positive schemata of the self and lead to disqualifying the experience (e.g. 'It's only a job to them, they are too smart and unable to understand or accept me' etc.). We will explore this in more detail in chapter 7. The point is, then, that transference beliefs and experiences sometimes need to be addressed so that the client is able to internalize the positive qualities of the therapeutic relationship.

*The dimension of control*  Helping clients gain control over feelings and internal meaning can be worked with as 'developing the positive or developing strength and ability'. This can lead to increased self-efficacy and self-acceptance. Hence control is not only about reducing dysfunctional behaviour and attitudes but also developing positive attributes.

*Power*  Related to control is power; that is, the ability to see oneself as being able to influence outcomes, especially interpersonal ones. Power is different from control in that one may not be able to control an outcome as one would like, but this does not mean one is powerless. There are things one can do to exert choice over the outcome. For example, a suicidally depressed man felt very angry with how his employers had responded to his time off work; they wanted him to resign. While he was preoccupied with the unfairness of it and the need to fight them, he felt powerless, overwhelmed and subordinate to them. Once he accepted that there was in reality little he could do (after talking to his union), he began to explore how he could turn it into an advantage, to see if he could get redundancy pay, which he successfully negotiated. He did not have to control the outcome in order to exert power in the situation and try to gain some advantage. Key cognitions here were, 'I must not let them treat me this way. If I do I am a weak, useless person.'

Also involved can be turning what is seen as a weakness into a strength. For example, the above person had hated his job but felt he had to stay in it to prove himself. Thoughts of moving on were seen as weak, an escape and an admission of defeat. Reconstruing escape as a strength and a sign of flexibility was helpful and counteracted feelings of powerlessness. In other words, if one has tried to make something successful and it does not work out then leaving and finding a new opportunity is useful. It is the cognitions that one has to prove oneself or that leaving a difficult situation is a sign of defeat, weakness, inadequacy or inferiority, that is often inhibiting. These cognitions often produce the feelings of entrapment and depression. Much depends on the case, however. In some situations it may in practice be very difficult to change a situation. In other cases, a depressed client may not have really tried to make a success of a situation or relationship thinking it would fail from the outset.

*Noting the valued attributes*   When clients are depressed they often exclude their positive attributes. For example, a client felt bad because of anger. So we made a list of all the negative attributes and hurt, and alongside made a list of all the positive attributes. In the positive list were things like, 'I try to care for others, I'm a loyal person, I don't purposefully cheat others. Others often turn to me for advice. I'm approachable.' This enabled him to see that while there were things he did not like about himself there were also things that he did value in himself and that he was disqualifying these attributes. Also we looked at anger as secondary to disappointment. The counsellor may look to see how the client can increase the list of positive attributes. All human beings need some degree of pride and respect (Gilbert, 1992) and helping clients see these qualities can be helpful, especially if they are validated by the counsellor and mirrored.

*All that I am*   Sometimes clients see their depression as more real, i.e. having cognitions like 'This is the real me.' Here it is useful to discuss the fact that in all of us we have the potential for becoming depressed and outline the typical internal beliefs that go with depression. Depression is no more or less real than joy, happiness, love, compassion, interest, humour or other internal experiences. Humans are mosaics of possibilities and feelings. Hence the counselling changes the construct from 'This is the real me' to 'This is only one part of my inner, human potential.' Again, the counsellor is indicating the complexity and variety of internal experience and breaking up black–white thinking about the self.

*Growth* Although it is painful, some clients can turn their depression into an opportunity for growth and becoming better than before (Gut, 1989). Here the counsellor draws attention to their increased insights and understanding, their new skill for controlling depressed feelings, and so on. One may ask 'What has your depression taught you; how have you changed?' This turns depression as a weakness (and shameful) into depression as an opportunity. However, these aspects normally come when progress is well under way. In the early days a person may see nothing positive in being depressed and it is not a good idea to explore this too early in counselling.

Jung pointed out that sometimes we become disturbed because we have failed to engage a developmental challenge. We cling to old ways of thinking and behaving because they seem safe. Thus change can be seen and discussed as a developmental challenge, a chance to move forward and grow. Sometimes clients come through a depression not just to return to their old premorbid styles but to change in major ways.

*Maturation* It has become clear in the past decade that in many ways cognitive counselling can aid maturation. This occurs because as a person changes in counselling, they are not just reprogramming themselves, but gaining deeper insight into the causes and origins of their self–other experiences and judgements. They may become more trusting of others and less critical of themselves. In ways that research is yet to make clear, there can be a more integrated sense of self that emerges out of the counselling experience. With maturation, attitudes and schemata become more flexible and varied. There is an evolution and growth of the self (Kegan, 1982). There has been a growing recognition that sometimes clients are not at a sufficiently developed stage in their maturation process to cope with complex interventions and the counsellor needs to have some awareness of this (Beck et al., 1990). Also efforts are being made to integrate cognitive approaches with developmental concepts derived from Piaget and Erikson (see Mahoney and Gabriel, 1987; Freeman et al., 1989). These efforts now represent different schools of cognitive counselling, e.g. the rationalists and the constructionists. Mahoney and Gabriel (1987) offer a good introduction to these issues.

## Concluding comments

This chapter has attempted to give an overview of the various types of interventions that are possible with depressed clients. The central points we have covered include:

1 Understanding the model and the way of working cognitively for change. This is by helping a client gain insight into, and take responsibility for, his/her cognitions.
2 The role of self-monitoring to increase awareness and to catch thoughts as they happen.
3 The importance of providing opportunities for re-evaluating experiences and situations: the process of re-education. This includes looking at the evidence, generating alternatives and, for depression especially, self-downing cognitions.
4 The role of behavioural practice, homework and social skills training, and also the importance of developing new social and interpersonal behaviours. The way we behave with others is influenced by our interpretations of interpersonal situations.
5 Counselling is not just about disputing the negative but also about facilitating the development of positive schemata and attitudes to the self. It is about growth.

Blending all these possibilities into skilful counselling takes time and practice. Many of these basic interventions are not achieved in five minutes but can take hours of work and repetition. They offer powerful means by which we can engage a depressed person's self-experience and help him/her shift out of these states of mind. However, as will be noted again in chapter 8, clients are not socially decontextualized and the environment can be a powerful recruiter of negative self-beliefs.

# PART II: THE APPLICATION OF COGNITIVE INTERPERSONAL COUNSELLING

## 5

## Beginning and Engaging the Depressed Client

Having outlined the main concepts of the cognitive-interpersonal approach to depression, we can now look at how these can be incorporated and crafted into a counselling relationship, starting with an overview of certain aims of counselling:

### Basic aims

1 Developing rapport.
2 Exploring possible fears, concerns and expectations of coming for counselling.
3 Shared understanding and meaning.
4 Exploring the story and eliciting key themes and cognitive-emotive styles:
   (a) taking a historical perspective;
   (b) working in the here and now.
5 Sharing therapeutic goals.
6 Explaining the counselling rationale.
7 Increasing awareness of the relationship among thoughts, feelings and social behaviour.
8 Challenging and moving to alternative conceptualizations.
9 Monitoring internal feelings and cognitions, and role enactments.
10 Homework and alternative role enactments.

Making this kind of list is helpful for clarification but should not be taken too literally as marking any set stages. For example, building a therapeutic alliance goes on throughout counselling. It commences when the person enters the room and is still important when it comes to saying goodbye. Secondly, all therapies have a certain course. Generally we speak of beginnings, middles and endings/termination. Beginnings are taken up with getting to know the client and the nature of the current difficulties, but also the client needs to get to know you. Different clients move through these stages at different paces and they often overlap. Some clients will move through the early stages very quickly, others less so. In this chapter our main concern is to explore the early part of counselling – beginnings and engagement.

Your interpersonal style will help to put the person at their ease and create a place of safety. Your style needs to be responsive to the client. Over-formality with very affiliative clients, or over-friendliness with more rigid personalities, is not comfortable for them. Different types of counselling will proceed in different ways. The client needs to know the kind of role relationship they will share with the counsellor. For example, some therapies are relatively free-floating and discursive, whereas others are directive and structured (Dryden, 1990). Cognitive approaches attempt to include the best of both free and directive approaches. Space is given to clients to explore and gain their own insights and generate their own solutions. This is conducted within the basic structure of the cognitive approach.

## Developing rapport

The process of developing rapport and eliciting a depressed client's interest in the possibility of change can be one of the most difficult. However, the techniques of change cannot be used without a good collaborative alliance. Indeed, many have cautioned against the tyranny of technique. Some cases of counselling fail because rapport and a good working relationship are not established. Resistance can be sometimes traced back to this early stage. Clients may not have felt understood, there may be various, unaddressed shame issues, and/or the client feels that the counsellor is pressuring them to change. Even a mild degree of relief early in counselling can help to build the therapeutic alliance. The important aspect here is that the client gains a sense of advocacy; that is, of someone who is going to work with them, and take their views and feelings seriously.

Also, it is the counsellor's role to do what he/she can to put the client at ease and acknowledge the asymmetrical nature of the role relationship. Depressed clients often have an acute sense of powerlessness and inferiority. Although one might not feel oneself to be personally threatening, this does not mean that the depressed client will experience you as unthreatening. Interpersonal social skills, such as smiling, taking an open posture and maybe offering a coffee may be reassuring. We should also pay attention to context. Try to create a relaxed atmosphere by attending to the setting. Comfortable chairs without an intervening desk are essential. Dress reasonably conventionally so that one's presentation is neutral without being overly formal or too 'way out'.

## Fears and concerns in coming to counselling

When many of us seek help for the first time there are various hopes and fears of the first attendance. One can create an opportunity to discuss various thoughts and feelings the client may have about coming to counselling: what are their explanations and expectations? After initial introductions, the counsellor may discuss the nature of the referral or the way the person came to take up counselling. Early in the first interview they might then ask various questions. For example, one might ask 'Before we start to discuss things in more detail, I wonder if we could look at what has been going through your mind about coming here today.' Here are some typical thoughts and feelings that might arise:

1 I was told to come (by general practitioner, spouse, friends).
2 I thought I had to do something.
3 I do not want to have to take drugs.
4 I want you to tell me what to do.
5 It's pointless, there is nothing to help me.
6 I doubt that you will understand me.
7 I expect you'll tell me it is my fault and to pull myself together.
8 You might discover I am a weak or bad person or a hopeless case.
9 I want to come but my spouse does not. (Hence, there may be various efforts to sabotage the counselling process at home. The counsellor may suggest bringing spouses or family members to counselling.)

Whatever the fears and doubts about engaging in counselling the counsellor tries to clarify them and bring them into the open, but does not engage in detailed discussion because, at this point, the client will have no evidence to judge how they are going to get on with you, how the counselling will be structured, or how useful it will be. So it is put to one side but not forgotten. If the depressed client has strong fears or doubts about coming for counselling, the counsellor may say something like 'I see your concerns. At this point, since it is early days, perhaps we could see how this session goes and review the situation as we go.'

Many of the basic fears of the depressed person relate to shame. So, early in counselling fears of being seen as inadequate, weak or bad can be addressed. We will be looking at shame later but in many cases it is not far from the surface and the counsellor should be mindful of this.

Nonverbal and verbal communication is often aimed at reassurance and offering unconditional positive regard, but this is something the client has to experience during counselling before they may feel safe enough to explore shame issues. Shame is one of the biggest blocks to developing a therapeutic relationship and therapeutic alliance. There is no quick solution to it and it is the basic attitude of the counsellor that determines if the content of shame can gradually emerge. For example, a client may know what the central issues are (e.g. previous sexual abuse; feeling that they are a fraud; or that underneath they feel deeply resentful and vengeful). However, they are too frightened (shame prone) to discuss them for fear of what the counsellor will think. In these cases the depressed client and counsellor can get into a kind of shadow dance of skirting around central issues. One should not assume that clients are prepared to reveal their central problems simply because they have presented themselves for help. For example, a client mid-way through counselling, when a central issue of aggressive, envious fantasies had been discussed said, 'You know, when I first came here I knew in my heart what I needed to talk about but just felt too ashamed to say. As we went through our first session I knew it was pointless because I couldn't tell you about it. That's what made me feel hopeless about this counselling. During each session we got close and I backed away and afterwards got so angry with myself and you for avoiding the issue.'

The client had expected that the counsellor would condemn these feelings, as had occurred in childhood. The counsellor accepted the client's anger for not being able to deal with it earlier and said simply that these feelings had been very painful for her to carry alone. So feelings of hopelessness can arise because the client has a secret agenda but is too fearful to reveal it. This is why the approach should be gentle and why trust is something that grows. The problem here is that early on the client has no experience of the counselling on which to make judgements and so it is not helpful to try to reassure the client with platitudes. Most clients prefer looking at the evidence approach rather than efforts to reassure them when they know perfectly well that they have not told the whole story, and therefore the counsellor cannot possibly know what is actually on their mind.

The counsellor should also beware of telling clients that 'You will need to trust me' or 'I can't help you unless you trust me.' No one is going to develop trust by instruction! Second, having a client reveal something shameful or something they have not told anyone else can feel like a positive validation of the counsellor and put them in a privileged position. However, beware of an eagerness to 'get the client to talk'. This can be experienced as intrusion and is not helpful. Beware the counsellor who boasts of how their clients reveal to them.

Other behaviours that help to develop rapport with the client and to overcome the fears of coming for counselling are those core skills outlined in chapter 1. The key issues in beginning the process of counselling are as follows:

---

Key issues 5.1   Beginning the process

1 Be aware of the power issues of counselling and try to create a safe place, e.g. friendly and open.
2 Give an opportunity to discuss fears of coming to or undertaking counselling.
3 Avoid providing false reassurances or making control statements, e.g. you must trust me.
4 Be aware that trust builds from experience.
5 Be aware that a client might have secret things they wish to talk about but are too ashamed.

---

**Shared meaning**

Sometimes we can look too hard for the important information and miss the obvious that presents with little effort. Even in very brief discussions early in counselling, key themes and concepts can be present. For example, the key theme that the counsellor will find out something bad about them may be a central issue in counselling (e.g. the fear that others will reject them if they get too close). So it is not always the case that key themes are 'deeply hidden'.

After the initial discussion of the thoughts and fears of counselling, the counsellor may begin to start to explore the current situation and what has brought the client into counselling. Counsellors differ on this. In my approach I might spend some time exploring basic symptoms and perhaps go through a Beck Depression Inventory (Beck et al., 1979). Part of feeling understood is that the client has been given an opportunity to tell how bad things are, such as sleep disturbance or loss of energy. The counsellor may then ask which of the symptoms causes most distress, with the aim of coming back to them at the end of the session and targeting the symptoms with some specific interventions. The counsellor must make contact with the reality of the client's experience. If sleep disturbance (say) is the most troubling symptom to the client, and the counsellor does not address this, then the client may feel that the counselling is not in tune with their experience.

By the end of this stage the counsellor and client will have shared the reasons for the referral, the feelings about attendance and the basic symptomatology and experiences of being depressed. It is now possible to move to the next phase of exploring the story.

## Exploring the story

At the start of obtaining the story the counsellor may need to be directive and use closed questions to begin the process. Below we will use the case of a client we will call Peter.

> *Counsellor:* We have spoken a little about your feelings of coming to counselling and the symptoms you are experiencing. Perhaps we could start to look at what's been happening to you recently.
> *Peter:* Yeah. Things seem to have been piling on top of me. I feel washed up, like there is no point any more.
> *Counsellor:* How long has that feeling been with you.
> *Peter:* Oh, I don't know, maybe a year. Maybe longer.
> *Counsellor:* What about before that? Looking back two years, how were you feeling then?
> *Peter:* Well, not like this. Things seemed to be going okay then.
> *Counsellor:* So you have been feeling low for about a year, but before that things seemed okay.
> *Peter:* Yes.
> *Counsellor:* Has there been anything that has happened over this year that seems to be related to this feeling low?
> *Peter:* Well, there isn't one thing. It's a number of things.
> *Counsellor:* A number of things? Could you tell me about them?
> *Peter:* We were hoping to move to a new house about a year ago and then we ran into financial difficulties. Then there was a problem at work. I didn't get the promotion I was due and all our plans started to slip away. My wife and I started to argue and I got pretty irritable. It seemed nothing was going right for me.
> [*The client then explained various life events, how they had happened and so forth*].
> *Counsellor:* So you have had a pretty rotten time recently. There seems to have been a number of disappointments for you.
> *Peter:* Yes, you could say that.

Once the counsellor has a general idea of life events (which in reality will take a lot longer than outlined here), he/she may wish to focus the discussion and share the difficult problems. A common cognitive concern is to go with the worst case or worst fear.

*Counsellor:* Looking at each of the disappointments, which one seems to have affected you most.

*Peter:* Well, right now it is my relationship with my wife. We were quite close early on like, but now we seem to be drifting apart. In a way I know it's me. I think I've messed it up if I'm honest.

*Counsellor:* So it's your relationship with your wife?

*Peter:* Yes, we argue a lot. She doesn't understand how I feel about things. She tells me we'll be okay and that I am making mountains out of molehills. I try to explain but she doesn't want to listen.

This is a rather common theme in depression and tells the story about feeling misunderstood and not receiving empathy from loved ones. Here we see the client oscillating between 'I've messed it up' and 'She doesn't want to listen.' The counsellor should also be alerted to the possibility that the client may fear that the counsellor will turn out to have a similar attitude (i.e. they won't listen). This theme needs empathic handling. If one rushes in too fast with techniques, the client can get the idea that 'Just like others, the counsellor thinks I am being irrational.'

Sometimes clients can present with a more angry style. For example, 'I keep trying to explain how I feel to others, my GP and so on, but they don't seem to listen.' One response might be 'So you feel that people who you are looking to for help, don't listen to you.' In other words, some kind of reflection of feelings of frustration can be useful. Unhelpful responses are 'Well, you haven't told me' or 'I can't help you until you tell me your difficulties.' These are defensive responses by the counsellor.

Let us return to Peter who has conflicts with his wife. The underlying theme is feeling that others do not appreciate his internal struggle and difficulty. Now at this point the counsellor has a choice. The counselling may become focused on historical data, or counselling may proceed to explore the meaning of the wife's behaviour for the client. Let us look at both options.

## Historical data gathering

*Counsellor:* If I understand you, some of your depression now revolves around the thought that your wife doesn't want to know about your worries and fears. We might call that a key issue for you right now. I wonder if we could just look at that in more detail for a moment. Have you had these kinds of ideas before?

*Peter:* Well, thinking about it, it has often seemed that way. As a child my parents had a lot of financial problems and were always rowing and there was never much time for us kids. I mean they tried and all that, but if we had problems they didn't really want to know.

*Counsellor:* Hm, this early feeling of others not having time for you and it being tied up with money difficulties may be important. Could we stay here a little and see how things were for you as you grew up?

The counsellor can then explore systematically the following key relationships:

1 Relationship with mother.
2 Relationship with father.
3 The relationship between mother and father.
4 Relationships with siblings.
5 Peer and school relationships.
6 Early dating relationships.
7 Marital relationships.
8 Relationships with children.
9 Other significant relationships, e.g. with grandparents, uncles, aunts or teachers.

As one moves through the life history, the counsellor is constantly checking on two things. First, repetitive patterns (e.g. of rejection, neglect, abuse or over-protection or needing to look after significant others). Second, the counsellor is interested in the attitudes that may have developed in these relationships by asking questions such as: what did you make of that?; what did that mean to you?; what sense did you derive from that?; what did you conclude from that?' For example:

> *Counsellor:* What was your relationship with your mother like?
> *Peter:* Well, I felt sorry for Mum. She had too many problems. Dad wasn't that interested really. He was more in the background. He worked hard and then spent a lot of time with his mates down the pub. He'd whack us if we were naughty but not show much interest.

The client then went on to reveal various ideas that others were generally unavailable to him, that his fears and concerns were not taken seriously and, importantly, that nobody could see things from his point of view. We were able to crystallize this basic theme as lack of recognition and that he had been very concerned through his life to gain recognition. So it began to make sense how the problems at work (failing to get the promotion), and those with his wife, were related to the underlying theme of lack of recognition and the associated disappointment.

The interpersonal school of cognitive counselling (Guidano and Liotti, 1983; Liotti, 1988; Safran and Segal, 1990) views early attachment relationships as important to the subsequent experience of self and others and the source of key attitudes. Sometimes clients may have highly idealized attitudes to parental figures. Here the basic theme can be of attempting to win parental approval but of feeling they have failed to do so and are not good enough. Evidence suggests that there is a tendency for depressed clients to have experienced their parenting as low on warmth and high on control. Some depressives have experienced very authoritarian parenting. This shapes their basic experiences of others, especially those in authority. In such cases, shame-proneness can be particularly pronounced and fears of put-down and being controlled become apparent in the counselling relationship. As a consequence, the depressed client may have learned various tactics to cope with parental style: (a) to be submissive and avoid trouble; (b) to try to achieve in an effort to impress others and win approval; (c) to put the needs of others first at the expense of themselves (perhaps more common in women); (d) to be aggressive and ensure that they control others (perhaps more common in men).

Other key issues can involve sibling rivalry and competitiveness (Fennell, 1989). Obtaining an outline of basic experiences and attitudes to significant others will be important in depressed clients, and it helps a client begin to comprehend how their depression may be the result of basic attitudes and experiences that existed before the depression (Gut, 1989; Safran and Segal, 1990). Sharing these experiences can aid rapport and heighten the experience of being understood, of having shared something of one's life with the counsellor.

Sometimes acknowledgement of the basic themes in a life history can arouse strong emotions. For example, consider Susan discussing her relationship with her mother:

*Susan:* My mother was cold. If we hurt ourselves she would say not to be a sissy and to get a grip. I can't really remember her ever hugging us that much or showing that she cared. If I see things on the TV where a mother and child get together and love each other or something, it really fills me up.

*Counsellor:* [*pausing and watching to see if this idea is starting to activate significant affects for the client. The counsellor gets the feeling of something she is struggling with.*] Maybe that feeling of filling up taps into something you would like, a kind of recognition of some deep hurt?

*Susan:* [*eyes beginning to water*] Oh yeah, [*pause*] yeah.

*Counsellor:* [*pause and gently*] Could you tell me what is going through your mind right now?

*Susan:* Your words of deep hurt. Like it is real deep, maybe too deep.

*Counsellor:* Too deep?

*Susan:* Yeah, too deep.

*Counsellor:* Like it's beyond reach?

*Susan:* Yeah, I guess so.

*Counsellor:* That's sounds like a hopeless, empty feeling.

*Susan:* [*cries and nods*].

In this situation the counsellor has used his empathy and been able to tap into a theme of emptiness and loss that is very charged with affect. However, the hopelessness aspect is related to ideas of it being too deep and beyond reach. Later Susan changed this to 'beyond repair'.

This example demonstrates that even in the first session, if one explores historical data, one may tap a highly charged affect related to basic beliefs and memories. As in Susan's case, these can often be associated with a certain kind of hopelessness of things being too late or beyond reach and repair. The counsellor may have a real sense of the need and emptiness of the client. At these times the experience of being understood and sharing that affect is important. The empathic response is one of being with the client rather than trying to do something to the client. Strong affect can stir up various feelings (e.g. to rescue) in the counsellor, but one should be cautious of defending against this affect with platitudes, or switching immediately to cognitive reconstruing.

On the other hand, a client might reveal a horrific story (say, of abuse) with little or no affect. Here the counsellor notes the absence of affect and may draw attention to this later. However, working with what has been called 'split off' affect is more complex than we can outline here (see Greenberg and Safran, 1987).

In exploring these issues the client can begin to build a picture of how previous experiences have led to various basic themes and self-schemata. Recall that during the historical exploration the counsellor asks 'What did this mean to you?' Here one is interested in how the self-structure has developed. Let us stay with the case of Susan:

*Counsellor:* You were saying that you felt your mother rarely hugged you, and this has given you the feeling that maybe things are beyond repair. Could I ask you to focus on that feeling for a moment and tell me what you have concluded about yourself.

*Susan:* Now or then?

*Counsellor:* Well, both really. Let's think about then, like when it was happening to you.

*Susan:* I'm not sure. I saw that other parents seemed to hug their kids and wondered why it was different at home. I guess in the back of my head I began to think maybe there was something wrong with me.

*Counsellor:* Something wrong with you?

*Susan:* Like she didn't love me because I was unlovable.

*Counsellor:* Did you have any ideas about what it was that might be unlovable about you.

*Susan:* [*pauses and looks down*] I've never mentioned this to anyone before, but you know I was the second girl and I sometimes thought that maybe they wanted a boy rather than another girl.

At this point in our counselling we note that Susan has introduced two new ideas of (a) lovability, and (b) gender. The
counsellor could check on the evidence – because her mother
didn't hug her, why did that mean she didn't love her? Or, look
to see if she thought her sister had been treated differently. But
at this stage, this might cut across the flow of meaning and
sharing that is emerging. So the counsellor notes this connection,
continues to explore self-ideas and feelings, and later offers a
crystallization.

> *Counsellor:* So you had the impression that because your mother didn't
> hug you that much, and you saw it was different for other kids, that
> maybe this was because she didn't love you. And you also had the
> idea that maybe this was because she had wanted a boy rather than
> another girl.
> *Susan:* Yeah, that sounds close to it. Yeah.

During the counselling it was then possible to look at evidence
and (in this case) discover that mother was equally distant from her
sister. There was little evidence that mother wanted a boy.
However, her sister had coped with the mother's distance
differently, leading Susan to feel more inadequate in comparison
with her sister.

At this stage we have engaged historical data to explore basic
key themes in self–other relationships. This is part of developing
rapport and also exploring the basic life themes of the person's
story. It helps clients feel understood. Clients are not a set of
disconnected problems to which one can apply techniques *ad hoc*.
Rather, one needs to have a sense of the whole person, since
people live with their history and make sense of the present by
virtue of what has happened in the past (Liotti, 1988; Safran and
Segal, 1990). In other words, we learn to experience ourselves via
the interactions we share with others (Gilbert, 1992). Nevertheless, it is not always appropriate to go into detail over life
history. Also different schools of cognitive counselling have
different views on the value of historical work (Mahoney and
Gabriel, 1987). Thus one might prefer to work in the present,
though historical working is nearly always important because (a)
it helps to develop a sharing and closer relationship; (b) it often
makes clear certain underlying patterns and beliefs that might be
difficult to formulate or be aware of when working in the present
(e.g. Susan's view that for her mother she had been born the
wrong sex); and (c) it gives people a sense of perspective and
continuity with their lives.

*Working in the present*

Above, we noted how the counsellor had worked with Peter's present problems with his wife. However, this is only part of the current information. In cognitive counselling a very important concern is to gain information on how the client evaluates the self, since it is often negative self-evaluation that is particularly linked to depression. To elicit the central ideas of the self it is often helpful to focus on a specific example and create an inference chain:

> *Counsellor:* Peter, this theme of recognition is obviously important to you. However, I wonder what goes through your mind about yourself when others don't seem to recognize your feelings in the way you might wish.
>
> *Peter:* I'm not sure I understand what you mean.
>
> *Counsellor:* Right. Well, let's think about a particular example. Let's imagine that tonight you try to talk to your wife and she doesn't take much interest. What will go through your mind?
>
> *Peter:* Hm, I think I feel something like, she doesn't really care that much. I am being a nuisance to her and shouldn't feel this way.
>
> *Counsellor:* You shouldn't feel this way?
>
> *Peter:* Yes.
>
> *Counsellor:* What do you say about you? What are your feelings about you as a person?
>
> *Peter:* I feel maybe I am making mountains out of molehills. Then I think, God, I must be weak and stupid for getting into such a state about things. If I'm honest part of me starts to dislike myself and I feel pretty worthless, inadequate, but like I'm trapped.
>
> *Counsellor:* So then you have two sets of ideas and evaluations, one about others and one about you. First is the idea that your wife doesn't recognize you and that feels disappointing. You interpret this as evidence that she doesn't care. But also because you feel unrecognized you feel weak, stupid and worthless. Is that how it is?
>
> *Peter:* Yeah. I feel pretty much a failure really.

What has happened here is that the counsellor has taken a specific example of the problem, set it up for detailed exploration and elicited the typical constructions that Peter makes. If one has access to historical data then one might see this as a repeating theme. Note how the counsellor spells out the different self–other evaluations (by saying 'You have two sets of evaluations, one about you and one about others').

Let us review our thoughts concerning the key issues in sharing meaning and eliciting basic, repetitive themes:

Key issues 5.2 Sharing and basic themes

1 Explore the current events that have led up to the depression and which may be continuing.
2 Look at the most difficult situation, or go with the worst.
3 If working with historical data, explore past significant relationships of the client and how these took on certain meanings.
4 Attempt to identify basic interpersonal styles and beliefs.
5 Note critical events (past or present) that stir up strong emotions and try to illuminate key self–other beliefs, clarifying these with the client.
6 Note possible areas where there is an absence of affect and a detached attitude.
7 When working in the present, create inference chains and separate and clarify key self–other beliefs.

### Sharing therapeutic goals

Sharing therapeutic goals means establishing with the client an agreed focus for work, agreeing the potential for change:

*Counsellor:* So far, Peter, we have talked of some of the things that are bothering you right now and [*if appropriate*] we have looked a little at your early life. Do you think working on some of those issues would be helpful?

*Peter:* What do you mean?

*Counsellor:* Well, you mentioned that you get disappointed and angry when your wife does not recognize your feelings and that you then begin to get angry at yourself. Suppose you could learn another way of dealing with this situation that didn't lead you to feel bad about you or think of yourself as weak, would that be helpful?

*Peter:* Oh, yes, of course. If I could cope better I would be happier.

*Counsellor:* So that might be a useful start. Perhaps one goal of our work together might be to see if we can help you cope in a different way at home.

Thus, beginning to share therapeutic goals involves hypothesizing what would be helpful. Asking questions like 'Do you think it would help you if . . .?' or 'What do you think would be most helpful to you right now . . .?' allows the client to begin the process of working towards change. It is little use the counsellor heading off in a direction that has not been agreed with the client (e.g. well I suggest we do this, or you do that). Although depressed clients often appear compliant, compliance is not the same as collaborative work. It is the skill of the counsellor to guide the client towards goals that are workable and seen as helpful, and to recognize the difference between compliance and collaboration. Sometimes this takes much therapeutic effort.

As mentioned earlier, in self psychology (Kohut, 1977; Wolf, 1988), cognitive counselling (Beck et al., 1979) and also rational emotive counselling (Ellis, 1977b) the counsellor pays particular attention to the self-experience and cognitions. In cognitive counselling this is called self-downing. In a case like Peter's we would be cautious about moving too quickly to dispute the fact that his wife does not care, without first attending to self-attacking and self-experience. There is no hard evidence that this is necessary, but it is my clinical impression that it is. For example, imagine that you feel others have not treated you well. You would want to find someone who, although they may not agree or disagree, shows empathic understanding and does not rush into trying to convince you that you are being over-sensitive. Later, when you feel better about yourself, it will be easier for you to recognize this, if it's true. Nevertheless, the evidence that Peter uses to believe his wife does not care for him will need to be addressed.

So, at the end of this part of the session, the counsellor has agreed with Peter that work will proceed by looking at his own self-downing and self-critical attitude.

## Explaining the therapeutic rationale

As one moves through the first few sessions, and normally around the time of sharing therapeutic goals, the counsellor will introduce and educate the client into the rationale of the cognitive approach. Cognitive counsellors see this as important because it enables the client to understand and take an active part in counselling and to make the therapeutic goals more clear. We do not believe that a simple statement such as 'We are here to talk about your feelings' is enough. This seems to be an over-medicalization of counselling in which, while the counsellor may know what is going on, what to expect and the stages counselling will take, the client is left largely in the dark. Also, clients are helped if they learn that there are things that they can do to help themselves and that the counsellor will offer guidance on this. Whatever model is used in counselling it is important that clients should be educated into the kind of process it will follow. Introducing the model can go something like this:

> *Counsellor:* We agreed just now that if you could find ways of helping you tackle this problem without 'attacking yourself' this might be helpful to you. Can I show you how we might approach this? [*At this*

*point the counsellor explores the client's interest.*] We call this a cognitive approach. We will focus on the meaning you give to events. A simple way to show this is for me to write an example with you and then look again at your current situation.

Following this, one takes a pad and pencil and, if necessary, moves one's chair to be at the side of the client. The counsellor draws out the four ABCD columns and runs through some simple example (e.g. the one given in chapter 3 of the noise in the kitchen). Following this, check that the client understands the approach. Does it make sense? Usually, the simple act of sitting next to the client and engaging in a shared task helps the sense of collaboration. However, if a person is very depressed this may be inappropriate, or if the client gives off various nonverbal signals of lack of interest, then one has to slow it down. So, while you are sharing the model, attend to the client's verbal and nonverbal behaviour and check on any thoughts they might be having (e.g. it is too logical, it won't help my feelings). However, assuming that the client agrees, one then moves to use the client's example.

> *Counsellor:* Okay, Peter, you have mentioned that problems with your wife seem to be central right now. One way we can explore this is to begin to make sense of how you think about these interactions. So we can write down together the typical sequence of events, thoughts and feelings.

For Peter it went like this:

> A = telling wife about how I feel and my worries about money but she tells me not to worry.
> C = anger, withdrawal and depression.
> B = she doesn't understand me.
> If she cared for me she would try to listen to me.
> You have to take the responsibility for worrying.
> You should be able to cope with this.
> You must be a pretty weak sort of person for not being able to cope.
> You are not worth caring for. You are worthless.

Notice that sometimes a client will talk to themselves as if talking to another (e.g. you should, you must, you are etc). Now this is quite common in depression and suggests a basic split in the experience of the self (Greenberg, 1979; Greenberg et al., 1990; Gilbert, 1992). One should notice this for it points to potential ways of intervening later (e.g. the two chairs approach in chapter 4; Greenberg, 1979).

In helping clients write thoughts down in this way a number of things are happening. First, it helps to crystallize those half-formed ideas in the mind and to clarify meaning. Second, it helps in the process of shared understanding, and offers a focus. Third, and rarely mentioned in the literature, there is a behavioural exposure aspect to this approach in that the thoughts and their affects are subjected to repeated exposure, challenge and desensitization.

## Increasing awareness

Once the client has understood the approach, the counsellor has many choices of how to increase awareness and challenge dysfunctional thoughts. These were outlined in chapter 4. The counsellor can begin to challenge the thoughts one by one; for example, by looking at the evidence for the thought, and/or exploring alternatives. Alternatively, the counsellor might use the friend technique to challenge the whole inference chain. In later sessions, the two chairs might be used. Also counsellor and client can work down the chain or up the chain. My preference is to work up the chain, to tackle the worst thing first, which is self-attacking and poor self-experience.

One also wishes to put across the idea that internal meanings (thoughts and personal constructions) are fuelling the dysphoric emotions. This is an educational aspect. Hence one may stop at this point and draw out the inference chain and emotions in a circle. The circle for Peter is shown in figure 5.1.

> *Counsellor:* Do you see how this sequence of events and ideas drive this circle around, such that you end up feeling worse until eventually you withdraw and go to bed. We could probably draw another circle that puts in the fact that when you withdraw, your wife also withdraws more, and so again things get worse for you.
> *Peter:* Now that you draw it out like that it seems so clear. That's exactly what happens. But I still can't see how it's going to change.

In this case writing down and drawing has helped the client clarify the issues. At these times one can check on the level of agreement and the possibilities of 'yes but' thinking.

> *Counsellor:* Okay, Peter, this is an important part of our work together, to gain more understanding of what goes through your mind, why, and how what goes through your mind makes things feel even worse.

At this time one begins to encourage the client to start to monitor his/her own thoughts and behaviour inside and outside counselling. One might give them thought recording forms that have two or more columns (see chapter 4), or one might write the key thoughts and attitudes on a card and ask the client to monitor how often he/she has these thoughts between sessions. In the early days try to keep it simple.

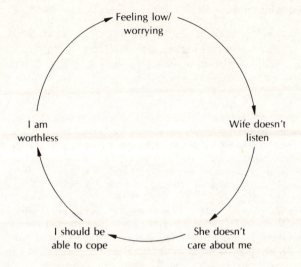

Figure 5.1 *The inference chain and emotions in Peter's case.*

Let us now review our thoughts regarding the key issues in sharing therapeutic goals, explaining the rationale and increasing awareness.

---

Key issues 5.3   Sharing and explaining the therapeutic process

1 Once a key set of dysphoric attitudes has been identified, use questions to explore what might be helpful, e.g. 'What would be helpful to change?'; 'Would it help if you could . . .?' etc.

2 Gain the client's cooperation in targeting certain cognitions or behaviours, i.e. agree therapeutic goals.

3 In depressed clients, look for the self-attacking and self-undermining cognitions.

4 Be clear about how you are to work together. Write things down, offer examples.

5 Use various procedures, e.g. writing down an inference chain and drawing circles of interacting thoughts and behaviours.

6 Prepare the client to begin to do this kind of monitoring for him/herself.

---

## Challenging and moving to alternative conceptualizations

To help develop alternatives we can work off the circle or go back to the chain. Self-attacking is often related to disappointment, and it is disappointment that activates the self-attack. It is important to help clients recognize this and reconsider and recognize their genuine emotions.

> *Counsellor:* What we can do now is to see if there are other ways that you might cope with this situation. Let's start with the idea that you are worthless. How does your wife not listening to you make you, a human being, worthless?
>
> *Peter:* Well, it doesn't I guess, it just feels that it does. [*Here the client has shifted the idea of worthlessness into a feeling so the counsellor can use this.*]
>
> *Counsellor:* Looking at it now does that feeling seem reliable?
>
> *Peter:* Well, logically no not really, but then that's how I feel.
>
> *Counsellor:* Well, right; you do feel bad but suppose it was something else other than worthlessness. What else might this bad feeling be?
>
> *Peter:* [*thinks for awhile*] Lonely, disappointed. [*pause*] Empty, I guess.
>
> *Counsellor:* Can you be in touch with those feelings for a moment?

The counsellor then stays here and explores images, feelings or memories enabling the client to gain deeper insight into how disappointment and emptiness launches the self-attack. Sometimes memories of being put down come to mind.

> *Counsellor:* Can you see how, when you feel unrecognized and disappointed and lonely, this triggers a self-attack and makes you think that you're worthless?
>
> *Peter:* Hm.
>
> *Counsellor:* Okay, so suppose we were to change that idea of worthlessness and stay with lonely and disappointed. How would that feel?
>
> *Peter:* [*pauses, thinking*] I would still feel upset but maybe not so angry with myself.

Later the counsellor might add:

> *Counsellor:* Well, it is possible that you learned to self-attack when you felt unrecognized as a child. Perhaps we can make some changes in this and help you develop a more accepting, caring attitude to yourself. It seems to me that the one time you need to care for you, like yourself, you put the boot in, a kind of kicking you when you're down.
>
> *Peter:* [*client smiles*] Oh, yeah, I've always been good at that.

Here the counsellor has attempted to shift the self-experience to a feeling of disappointment from a self-attack. Remember in chapter 2 we said that our relationships with ourselves can either be one of power or love. Here we try to turn the attacking self into a caring self. This is likely to need repetition many times since there is a long history of the experience of lack of recognition triggering the self-attack. Also note that sometimes we need to help clients experience specific affects more deeply. In these cases anger at self becomes a secondary emotion to disappointment and loss, especially in depression, and this linkage will need further work (see Wolf, 1988). The counsellor's empathy for the disappointment will be important in the healing process. From a cognitive point of view, a clear insight into the linkage of the affect of disappointment and anger at the self is helpful. Thus before moving to challenging, one can provide further opportunities for reflecting the client's experience of disappointment and loneliness.

> *Counsellor:* The feelings of disappointment are painful and you are not sure what to do with them.

This may lead to further discussion about how to cope with disappointment or historical events. It may also lead to attitudes like 'I have to be loved and recognized, otherwise it is terrible and unbearable.' Thus the experience of disappointment itself may be heightened by the client telling him/herself that they cannot possibly bear it. Following this the counsellor can move to more cognitive work.

> *Counsellor:* Let's think more about this idea of worthlessness. Now sometimes we might call this 'black and white' thinking, or 'either/or' thinking. Like if my wife recognizes me I am okay if not I'm worthless. Suppose you had a friend and one day he comes to you with a rather similar story what would you say to him?
> *Peter:* I'd understand his feelings I think.
> *Counsellor:* So you wouldn't say well, I'm sorry my friend, your wife doesn't share your fears therefore she doesn't care for you. You should be able to cope, therefore you are worthless.
> *Peter:* [*smiles*] Oh, no, I wouldn't say that.
> *Counsellor:* Would you think it?

Sometimes people would think harshly of others, although they would not say so and this needs to be recognized. The counsellor's response here can be, 'Well, you are certainly consistent. But if you did say it, how would your friend feel?', again getting across the idea that the attack leads to feeling worse.

At this point one again has a choice. We can continue to work the theme of worthlessness in various ways. We might talk about the little *i* and big *I* (see chapter 4), pointing out that we are made up of multiple bits, feelings, competencies, abilities and so forth and that the client is globally rating themselves negatively due to one situation or theme. We may talk about putting all one's eggs in one basket, or use the straight line. One could encourage the client to draw up a list of things that they can do which does not depend on the wife's recognition. Other possibilities involve distinguishing self from performance judgements (IT–ME), breaking up black–white thinking, the friend technique, advantages–disadvantages of maintaining them. In role reversal one might say 'How might you convince a friend who has a similar experience, that because his wife does not listen to his money worries this does not mean that she does not care for him or that he is worthless.' Re-attribution training can also be used; for example, can Peter generate alternative explanations for why his wife does not wish to listen to his worries? When Peter was asked this he said it was his wife's attitude to things, 'If you can't change it, worrying only makes it worse.' Thus we had an alternative explanation for his wife not wishing to focus on his money worries. This technique therefore involved Peter challenging his thoughts with 'What is the evidence that I am worthless because my wife doesn't listen to me? Maybe she just sees things differently' and 'Maybe she is worried too, but deals with it in a different way.'

To help clients learn how to challenge their thoughts, the counsellor may wish to offer hand-outs that have been specifically prepared for depressed people (e.g. Fennell, 1989). One can also suggest reading material (for example, an appropriate chapter in David Burns' book *Feeling Good* [1980]). This can then become a subject for discussion, although it is not a substitute for the actual counselling. One can also engage in more philosophical discussions and sometimes arrive at particular phrases that seem to appeal to clients. For example, with those who are socially dependent one can discuss the advantages and disadvantages of having others decide one's self-worth. And a challenge of counselling is 'to become the keeper of one's own self-worth'. One client came up with 'To want approval is natural, to rely on it is a pain.' The exact interventions depend on the case, but the basic intervention is to help break up the global self-attack and sense of worthlessness, to come to the rescue of the self.

By the end of this intervention the client will have an agreed set of alternative ideas to activate in situations of disappointment. Sometimes one can write these out on a flash card, on one side of which are the typical depressing thoughts, and on the other the agreed alternatives. Clients often like this because it links them back to the counselling situation when they are on their own and triggers memory of the session.

Often, because the counsellor has come in on the side of the self and has attempted to rescue it from internal attack and self-downing, while at the same time helping the client to acknowledge affects like disappointment, emptiness and so on, this can put the counselling relationship on a sound footing. From here, the client may be able to consider the way his wife is actually caring and to focus on what she does do rather than on what she does not.

Let us now review our thoughts about challenging and moving to alternative conceptualizations.

---

Key issues 5.4 Challenging and moving to alternative conceptualizations

1 Look for and clarify the negative self-beliefs and self-attacking in the depressed client's cognitive style.
2 Help the client to recognize the situations and feelings that often precede self-attacking, e.g. disappointment.
3 Be empathic to these feelings of disappointment in depression, which often centre on evaluations of how others treat the client.
4 Note ideas like 'I must be, I have to be recognized, otherwise it is unbearable and I am a worthless person.'
5 Use a variety of approaches to interrupt the disappointment – self-attack, self as worthless, sequence; e.g. looking at the evidence, focus on black–white thinking, or use the friend technique.

---

## Monitoring internal feelings and cognitions, and role enactments

A major aspect of all therapies is to increase awareness outside the counselling situation. There are a number of ways of doing this. One is to teach clients how to use dysfunctional thought records (Blackburn and Davidson, 1990). Some clients take to this very easily and find it helpful, others do not. Sometimes it is helpful to write out flash cards that they take out whenever they feel themselves slipping; this acts as a prompt. It is helpful to advise them to note any disconfirming ideas they might have. For example, a client would see the value of the card during counselling but when alone would discount it's validity, 'It's too rational; I can't change my ideas that simply.' The intervention here might be, 'Well, perhaps that is true but let's try for a while and see how it goes. What have I got to lose.'

Cognitive counsellors often talk about developing the observing self (Beck et al., 1985). It has been found that if depressed clients can distance themselves from their thoughts and look in on themselves, this is helpful. Hence the counsellor can suggest that: 'One part of the self that we are trying to develop is your observing self and your self-awareness. If we can help you identify ideas and images as they pass through your mind then we might have a better handle on helping to change them.' This process of increasing self-awareness via self-monitoring can be very helpful with some clients (Beck et al., 1985; Safran and Segal, 1990). Teaching self-awareness and increasing the activity of the observing self helps put a buffer between the thoughts and the affect associated with them.

### Homework and alternative role enactments

Cognitive counsellors believe that helping clients make changes in their actual social behaviour is more important than waiting for it to happen. This is the value of homework, which can be set up in a number of ways, but again it is engaging the client's collaboration that is important not their compliance. With compliance they may go through the motions of the homework but not really engage it. At the end of the session one gives a summary of what has taken place. This might be written down for the depressed client to take away and reflect on.

> *Counsellor:* We are coming to the end of the session now and I would like to go through what we have shared together. You started by telling me that things seem to have been worse for you over the past year, and that this is associated with a number of disappointments and financial worries. We looked a little at your early life and found that you have often had the idea that others didn't really have time for you. We then looked at a specific area that is causing you distress right now and this was to do with your relationship with your wife. Here we noted two key themes. The idea that your wife does not care for you because she tells you that you are making mountains out of molehills, and the idea that because of this you are weak and worthless. We also explored how these ideas go around in your mind making your distress even greater. [*pause*] Is that a fair summary?
>
> *Peter:* Yes, I think so.
>
> *Counsellor:* Okay, Peter, given what we have discussed can you think of anything you might like to try out between now and the next time we meet?

This involves helping clients to plan their own homework. This again is aimed at encouraging the client to collaborate actively in the process of change.

> *Peter:* I guess I have to practice not putting myself down when my wife doesn't want to hear about my problems.

*Counsellor:* How could you do that?

*Peter:* By being more aware, as you say, of my disappointment and not attacking myself when I feel disappointed.

*Counsellor:* Yes, that's right. Otherwise you have two problems. One is the disappointment and the other is the attack on you. [*Counsellor points to the circle and watches to see if Peter is thinking about it.*] So over the next week, can you keep a note of the situations that arise when this circle seems to be activated? Note down your thoughts and how you tried to cope with them. We can explore that in more detail next week.

However, the counsellor is also aware that helping Peter make changes in his social behaviour would be important both for him and the quality of the marriage. Thus, the counsellor explores the possibility of Peter taking on new roles within the relationship. In the case of role enactments it is helpful to enable the client to predict the social consequences of their behaviour.

*Counsellor:* You were also saying earlier that you and your wife get into arguments about things, especially your view on money, and you both withdraw from each other. Would it be worth trying not to engage this subject right now as it is such a bone of contention?

*Peter:* Oh yes, if I could stop doing that it would be much calmer at home. It really winds her up.

*Counsellor:* Well, shall we try for a week and see how it goes? You can bring your worries about money here and we will look at them together.

Here the counsellor has attempted to bring some relief to the marital situation by making the counselling the focus for his fears and worries. This is aimed at setting a new style in the relationship. At some point the partner might be invited to the counselling but at the moment it is helpful to see if the client can make changes himself. There may also be various resentments that will have to be worked with but these will come later.

The other area one might focus on is how they could share more positive relations. Could Peter take his wife out, e.g. to a film or on a walk? What were the things they enjoyed doing in the past? Thus increasing the level of mutually rewarding activities can be helpful. The counsellor can discuss how the depression can cause problems in marriage against one's true desires. Thus, looking at how a client might instigate a more positive role relationship can be important. But, of course, this depends on the case, and the client has to have a basic desire to continue the relationship. In cases where there is much resentment, and a desire to terminate the relationship, then working on shared activities may be counter-productive. There may be too much anger with the spouse to make this an attractive idea, at least early in counselling.

In these situations the couple may need to be brought together for marital counselling. In Peter's case the loss of the previously good relationship was another source of disappointment. Helping him focus on how he could improve it again was helpful to him and made him feel more in control.

Let us now review our thoughts and look at the key issues in homework and alternative role enactments.

---

Key issues 5.5   Homework and alternative role enactments

1 Help the client recognize that self-monitoring is part of homework and also a useful life skill.

2 Teach the client to monitor and test out cognitions between sessions and review this with him/her at the beginning of each session.

3 Help clients plan their own homework and behavioural experiments.

4 With depressed clients, these behavioural experiments often involve developing more rewarding social behaviour, e.g. seeing friends, or relating in a different way to a spouse.

---

**Concluding comments**

In this chapter we have looked at the basic introductions to counselling the depressed client and the importance of developing a therapeutic alliance (Dryden, 1989c) that is focused on the self and its internal relationship. In depression it is always useful to keep the self-relationship as the central issue. In this way the counsellor is less likely to get lost in various details of a client's difficulties. This does not mean that one ignores the interpretations of other people with whom one is interacting (Gilbert, 1992), instead it is fostering a self-belief system which is valuing and supporting rather than attacking and undermining. Homework, in the early stages, needs to be agreed as being helpful and achievable. It also enables a client to regain hope and control by increasing the level of positive rewardable behaviour.

# 6

## Helping Depressed Clients to Change: Some Basic Interpersonal Dimensions

This chapter explores the counselling process once counselling is underway. In general, there are some typical procedures that can help to give structure to sessions:

1 Checking on mood at the beginning of each session. Has it got worse, stayed the same or improved?
2 The counsellor will review homework or role enactment experiments outside counselling.
3 The counsellor will check for any critical events between sessions.
4 Feelings and ideas about previous sessions will be explored, e.g. 'Did you have any new thoughts this week arising from our last meeting?'
5 Together, counsellor and client will then set an agenda and priorities for the session.

The above occurs (usually) in the first ten minutes or so of the session. The structure should not be overly prescribed, however, as this may allow for avoiding key themes. A clue to this problem can be obtained if the client tends to leave the important material to the last five minutes. As counselling progresses more information will arise as to the key interpersonal areas that are problematic and these will tend to present as repetitive themes, e.g. need for approval/recognition, assertiveness etc. (Gilbert, 1992).

In this chapter we will explore how to work with some central self-schemata, beginning with approval. We will use the approach of advantages–disadvantages. Some cognitive counsellors ask clients to rate (in percentages or numbers) the degree of the advantage or disadvantage (e.g. see Blackburn and Davidson, 1990), but clients may see this as too intellectual. In the approach here we are more interested in the meaning and discussion of meaning.

## Approval seeking

Most theories of depression see (excessive) needs for approval as playing a central role in vulnerability and maintenance of depression (Gilbert, 1992). When approval seeking relates to an intimate domain this often takes the form of needs to confirm one's lovability and to stay in a close relationship with another (Beck, 1983). When approval needs operate in a less intimate domain, social approval needs are focused on recognition of talent and ability. These are, however, not mutually exclusive. Loss of needed, intimate relationships often involves the affects of yearning and proximity seeking. Those focused on more social domains do not involve the same yearning for proximity. In dealing with dependency, the counsellor should be clear about the distinction between genuine emotional dependency and other forms (e.g. economic). Often dependency is secondary to a feeling of inferiority. Here we look at a case of intimate dependency.

On the surface, Sally seemed to have a need for intense relationships with men and much reassurance once in them. She had become depressed when a long-standing relationship (with Fred) had broken down. She understood the basis of the cognitive approach and had made some early gains in her counselling. Nevertheless, on core issues she seemed rather stuck. At this point we used the advantages (gains) and disadvantages (losses) procedure to help articulate the difficulty. The following dialogue highlights how the counsellor can use a technique but must stay open to the affective changes that occur in the session.

> *Sally:* I just never seem to be able to make a success of relationships. I mean, I thought that Fred and I were doing okay but it ended like all the others.
> *Counsellor:* Did Fred tell you why he was breaking up?
> *Sally:* Well, he mentioned that maybe I was too intense. Like I needed too much reassurance. I wanted to be with him all the time. This seemed to me how lovers should be. I didn't like him looking at other women and, like I said before, we did sometimes have rows over this.

The counsellor might note the possibility of black–white thinking here, i.e. 'Either I am with a lover all the time or we don't have a loving relationship.' This is implied, if not stated clearly. For Sally, working on black–white thinking has only been marginally helpful.

> *Counsellor:* Do you think Fred had a point?
> *Sally:* Probably. Yes.
> *Counsellor:* Is that something we might continue to work on?
> *Sally:* Maybe, but I don't think I can be any different. I have tried

really, but I just seem to get taken over by the relationship, like it is everything to me.

*Counsellor:* Sounds like there are some basic ideas about changing and not being able to. What about if we look at the advantages and disadvantages of changing, or if you like the gains and losses. Perhaps we can get a clearer idea of what this is about. I'm going to draw two columns and call one 'advantages' and the other 'disadvantages'. Okay? [*Sally nods.*] Now, what would be the advantages of changing, becoming less intense and needy in the relationship?

*Sally:* Well, it would certainly make things easier I guess.

*Counsellor:* Okay, that's our first advantage. It would make things easier. Anything else?

*Sally:* I might hold onto my man.

[*The counsellor notes the words 'hold onto'. As we mentioned (chapter 3) key words can be markers for underlying basic beliefs.*]

*Counsellor:* You might hold onto a man. Any other advantages?

*Sally:* [*thinks*] No, can't think of any.

*Counsellor:* Fine, let's just stop here for a moment. Suppose you did find it possible to be less intense and needy, how would that affect you? I mean, what would be the benefits for you, how would you be different, like inside you? [*Here the counsellor is helping to focus more on the internal self-experience.*]

*Sally:* I wouldn't get so jealous.

*Counsellor:* Would that feel better?

*Sally:* Oh yes. I hate feeling jealous, it really cuts me up you know.

*Counsellor:* Okay, so becoming less jealous might be a help. Anything else, like how your thoughts or fantasies might go?

[*Note how the counsellor is having to draw out advantages with questions.*]

*Sally:* Oh, yeah, that. Yeah, I wouldn't spend so much time fantasizing or worrying about the relationship. Like I told you before, they kind of take me over and I spend all my time thinking about the relationship, mainly if it's going to work out and what will happen if it doesn't.

*Counsellor:* So if you became less intense and needy then you might have less worrying thoughts about the relationship. What about you? I mean how might you come to think about yourself – your own person-ness.

*Sally:* Hmm, I've been thinking about that since I saw you and talked to Jackie about it. I do feel bad about myself when things don't work out, like I've put so much effort into it and it goes wrong, so maybe it's me. I get confused with that.

*Counsellor:* What kinds of ideas do you have about you?

*Sally:* It's difficult to put into words but somewhere I feel I must be unlovable.

[*Note how the counsellor has had to ask more than once to help Sally get to her beliefs about herself when the relationship does not work. Then comes the idea 'maybe I'm not lovable.'*]

*Counsellor:* Are there any other thoughts or feelings about yourself?

*Sally:* I guess I'm angry with myself. I look back and see what I did wrong. I think of how I was jealous and at times demanding, and wish I could be more relaxed not so needy you know. Part of me would like to be more independent.

[*After further discussion on these general themes the counsellor summarizes.*]

*Counsellor:* Let's go over some of the advantages of becoming less intense. The relationship might be easier. You'd feel less jealous; you might be able to maintain the relationship; you might get less angry with you and feel better about yourself; you may become more independent. How does that sound?

*Sally:* Well, when you lay it out like that it sounds silly to get so involved and I suppose I do lose something.

*Counsellor:* [*smiling*] I think I see a 'but' on your face though.

*Sally:* You make it sound so logical but I can't help it. It's my heart that rules me.

Here Sally acknowledges the logic of change yet is not convinced. Counsellors should not be discouraged by this. Thus we must move to the disadvantages. Indeed, in working with depressed clients, helping them see the advantages of change may be less important than working with the disadvantages, thus spending more time looking at the disadvantages may be valuable. This turned out to be important in Sally's case.

*Counsellor:* [*smiles*] You're right, of course. We are approaching the issue in a reasonably logical way but our feelings don't always obey logic. Still, maybe as you say, you can see that it is not all gains in having an intense relationship. Anyhow we can come back to this. Let's focus on the aspect that you mention here again about being taken over by the relationship.

Now the counsellor has already explored inference chains on relationships and found that Sally's sense of feeling good about herself is very much related to having a man love her (i.e. close intimate relationships). She is also competitive in love, hence her jealousy. She has beliefs such as 'If a man loves me I must be as good or better than other women.' At the same time, however, she often feels vulnerable because this good sense of self can be taken away from her if the relationship fails. Sally has not been able to make a lot of progress with simple alternative thinking so the problem can be approached from a different direction and we can try to engage Sally more fully in understanding the benefits and losses to her of changing her basic attitudes.

*Counsellor:* So far we have looked at a few advantages of becoming less intense in relationships with men, but now let's think about the disadvantages. What would you lose?

*Sally:* The first thing that springs to mind, even as we were going through the advantages, was that it wouldn't be natural.

*Counsellor:* Natural?

*Sally:* It wouldn't be me, like I'd either be pretending or that I didn't care that much.

*Counsellor:* So it's the intense feeling that makes it seem real and natural?

*Sally:* Yes.

*Counsellor:* Okay, what other disadvantages are there?

*Sally:* I wouldn't be sure if this was the right man for me. Like I'd be wasting my time.

[*The counsellor thinks about the statement 'right man for me', and considers the possibility of looking at the evidence that emotions are the best way to make such judgements. However, at this point it is decided to focus on internal feelings.*]

*Counsellor:* How would you feel inside?

*Sally:* [*thinking*] Kind of empty about it, I guess.

*Counsellor:* Empty. Without the intensity it would feel empty?

*Sally:* I think so.

*Counsellor:* How about you? What would your experience of you be?

[*Again, note how the counsellor returns to the self-evaluation.*]

*Sally:* The same empty feeling.

At this point the client touches affect and her mood seems to become more sad. This is picked up in her nonverbal behaviour and slowed speech. These affective pointers (Greenberg and Safran, 1987) are important to stay with. So even though we are using a fairly structured technique we remain sensitive to the affective changes in the session.

*Counsellor:* That's interesting, Sally. Without the intense feeling in the relationship it feels empty and you feel empty in it. Can you remember having these feelings before, like in childhood?

*Sally:* [*Speech rate slows down and talks more deliberately.*] As I think about it, it reminds me of my Dad. Poor old Dad, he had to work long hours and was often away from home. I just got this image of waiting at the window for him to come home and then mother would say I'd have to go to bed or he wasn't coming home that night. I really used to miss him 'cos on the occasions when he was there he would spend a lot of time with me and it was really good, like really good and exciting. He'd take me out, unlike Mum. I hated him going away again, life seemed more dull. Later, they got divorced and secretly I really hoped I could go and live with him but Mum wanted us to stay with her. She needed us I suppose, but I wanted to be with Dad.

The client has spontaneously made a link with the past, noting various memories. Safran and Segal (1990) suggest that working with historical data is important, especially if explored in the course of counselling, in the presence of affect, and when it emerges spontaneously. Thus we cannot let this opportunity go by.

*Counsellor:* Sounds like he really liked being with you when he was home?

*Sally:* Sometimes I thought he enjoyed being with me more than Mum. They didn't get on at all. He didn't talk about it much but I always felt on his side.

*Counsellor:* Against Mum?

*Sally:* Yeah, perhaps.

The counsellor notes the possible competition with mother for father's affection. It runs through his mind that this might have something to do with her competitive style and preparedness to drop female friends whenever a man came along. But since the focus is on the need for intensity we stay with this theme.

*Counsellor:* Sounds like you longed for that intensity to be there all the time; to be with Dad.

*Sally:* [*nods sadly*].

*Counsellor:* Do you think those experiences might have anything to do with what happens with you today in relationships?

*Sally:* I'd never thought of that. [*Pause*] I can see that.

*Counsellor:* You look sad.

*Sally:* I was just remembering how lonely I used to feel and how much I wished he'd come home.

At this point, while using an advantages–disadvantages approach, we have tapped into an underlying memory of a need for intensity and closeness, and how there is both a desire to recapture closeness, and also a fear of losing it. In attachment theory (e.g. Liotti, 1988) this might be seen as an anxious attachment to father that has set a template for anxious attachment to men. However, the point is, there does seem to be some early schemata here and these are going to need work to help Sally change her interpersonal style with lovers.

It is important then that the counsellor does not use the techniques of counselling simply as 'techniques' but crafts them into a therapeutic relationship. They are not a recipe to help people understand at only a rational level the nature of their difficulties but also to engage emotional experience. So one wants to try to bring this emotional experience into the list of disadvantages.

*Counsellor:* Okay, Sally, perhaps we can see how this need for intensity may have something to do with your past experience with Dad. But I guess that this may turn out to be an advantage. I mean if some of the need for intensity is coming from a disappointing relationship with Dad, then it might be helpful to try to help with this disappointment rather than you carrying it from one relationship to another.

[*Here the counsellor is directing attention to Sally's interpersonal style.*]

*Sally:* I hadn't seen that, but sitting here it makes sense. Are you saying that I am trying to recapture something?

*Counsellor:* What do you think?

*Sally:* I think I have known that but yet haven't been aware of it. [*Pause*] Oh, that sounds silly doesn't it?

*Counsellor:* [*gently*] I wouldn't say silly at all. It seems more about making connections. Something we feel but like it's in the background, not clear.

*Sally:* Yes, that's how it is, in the background, not clear.

We then had a discussion of what we mean by 'being in the background' and how some of our ideas and feelings get connected within us without consciously recognizing it. In essence, Sally had a belief which said 'I must have a close relationship with a man to be happy.' This came from a real experience of being happy when she was close to her father.

*Counsellor:* So we are saying that a disadvantage of giving up the need for intensity may mean that you feel less able to recapture something, to use your words.

We spent about twenty minutes in emotional discussion around this theme trying to clarify it and articulate the basic beliefs. The focus remained the disadvantage of losing intensity in relationships with men. It is not only the connection with the past that was important here, but the link (with the memory) of intense emptiness and loss. At the end of this part of the session the counsellor returned to the basic task. We had both gained more insight into the feared losses associated with changing and giving up intensity. At times Sally's sadness was intense.

*Counsellor:* Okay, Sally, let's look on our paper and see what we've got here. First, you see that intensity in relationships is not all good now. Therefore you recognize some potential benefits from becoming less intense. I would direct your attention to your style of relating. However, there are many disadvantages in making this change. First, it may make the relationship feel unnatural or unreal and this links to a feeling of emptiness. That in turn reminds you of your relationship with your father. So, although at a logical level, you can understand that there are advantages to becoming less intense and needy, at an emotional level it does not feel like a gain, but a pretty big loss. Now nobody will change if they feel inside they are heading for a loss.

*Sally:* [*slightly tearful*] Yeah, I must say I have been trying to follow through in counselling but that has been the feeling. I know I want to change and part of me knows what we've been doing is sensible but inside I don't want to change, like I am leaving something important behind.

*Counsellor:* Do you think you are clearer about what you might be leaving behind?

*Sally:* The kind of relationship I wanted with Dad [*cries gently*].

At this point the counsellor is silent, allowing Susan to be aware of the pain of the insight. Later the counsellor emphasizes the belief 'I must have an intense relationship to be happy', and summarizes what has taken place.

As counselling progressed, Sally began to reach a certain anger at her father who had been idealized. She had not been able to contact this before because her positive feelings for him had been special and an important source of self-esteem. Now this is not at all uncommon in idealized relationships when there has actually been considerable loss and distance. Making contact with the anger can be helpful. It helped Sally understand that often, in intimate relationships, she also felt resentful without really knowing why. She began to explore the fear of being alone and left behind. Without intensity, she might be left like mother, alone and somewhat bitter. So again the techniques of counselling were ways of helping her gain insight and make important changes in self-understanding and interpersonal relationships. One of her homeworks was to try to look at ordinary friendships with men and the feelings she had about them. We also looked at other ways of evaluating what kind of relationship she wanted with a man, e.g. honesty, respect, sharing pleasant activities, etc.

As counselling progresses one is gradually weaving together various themes and illuminating basic schemata and memories, such that they become available for reworking in the present situation.

## Achievement

The need for achievement is also common in depression (see chapter 2). Let us look at Dan who showed this strongly. Dan had a need for approval, but it did not manifest as intimate or proximity needs as did Sally's. Rather it was a need to be recognized as talented and able. Let us now consider Dan using the same technique of advantages–disadvantages (gains–losses).

> *Counsellor:* You were saying earlier, Dan, that you felt a great need to achieve things and felt that much of your life had been a failure. Over the past few sessions we have looked at the evidence for this and also how you would talk to a friend. Has that changed things?
>
> *Dan:* I can see what you are driving at and it sort of makes sense. I do punish myself a lot but it's so automatic that it's difficult to change.
>
> *Counsellor:* Well, let's look at this from a different perspective for a moment. We can make a list of the gains and losses to changing the need for success. I'll come and sit next to you and we can write them out together. [*Does so.*] Now, let's look at the advantages first. What might be the advantages of changing this drive for success?

*Dan:* I would be more relaxed about things and less anxious.
*Counsellor:* Anything else?

The following advantages were then elicited. 'I'd be less hard on myself. I'd be easier to live with. If I was less tense I might get less depressed. Life might be more fun.'

*Counsellor:* Okay, let us now look at the disadvantages.

These were the disadvantages: I might become sloppy. I might end up lazy. Might lose respect (he took secret pride from others calling him a perfectionist. He also took secret pride from feeling superior to others). I might lose my purpose in life and life would become empty and pointless.

> *Counsellor:* It is understandable why you would find it difficult to change if these are the likely consequences. Counselling must seem a bit confusing to you if you think that by changing your style you are going to feel worse, like empty and pointless.
> *Dan:* [*long pause as Dan looks over the list*] Yes. That makes sense. I kind of know what you are saying but it has never seemed a right fit for me, like I was frightened of letting go of something. I have felt confused really.

From here counselling began to work more closely with the fears and the sense of superiority that Dan maintained for his perfectionism, and the fear of letting go. There was some mourning of the failure of recognition of early life and a movement to look at life with regard to more pleasurable activities. Black–white thinking was explored many times in terms of becoming more sloppy and losing respect. Each time we were able to keep in mind the fear of change.

In these cases the counsellor needs to empathize with the (sometimes desperate) feelings of need for recognition and to be valued. In cognitive terms this is the 'I must' beliefs. It is not the case that these clients want to be cared for or necessarily crave an intense intimate relationship. More often they are seeking a sense of personal value and have worked out various tactics for trying to achieve it. If the counsellor does not recognize this need for value and moves too quickly to challenge, the client can feel misunderstood. Further, the counsellor should be alert to the disappointment and grief of not having felt valued that goes with these themes. Counsellors can sometimes miss the difficult struggle for respect and a sense of personal value that have often been important life goals (see Gilbert, 1992, ch. 7).

In both Sally's and Dan's cases the counsellor often returns to self-evaluation. Why *must* you be loved or valued? Slowly the client can turn a must into a preference. The key is helping the person to avoid self-attacking or self-downing if the preferences do not come about. If one can stop the self-attacking and maintain a reasonably stable self-relationship, then depression might be less likely. This is a central focus of rational emotive therapy (see also Greenberg et al., 1990). Let us now review our thoughts about one of the most commonly used techniques: advantages–disadvantages.

---

**Key issues 6.1    Working on advantages–disadvantages**

1  The counsellor may have to draw out the advantages and help people to list these.
2  The counsellor uses questions to help clients articulate how they might think about themselves differently through changing.
3  It is common, however, that working with the advantages of change is not always helpful. People often know what might be in their best interests, but do not do it.
4  Consequently, looking at the disadvantages of change can be more powerful.
5  The counsellor can draw out the negative self-beliefs, self-experiences and basic fears and losses that might arise from change.
6  If clients spontaneously report memories or images from the past that are linked with negative emotions, the counsellor should explore these. Sometimes the advantages–disadvantages is the focus for the whole session.

---

**Assertiveness**

There is increasing evidence that assertiveness is often a problem in depression. Either, clients carry considerable resentment and then label themselves as bad for feeling resentful, and/or they tend to have explosions of anger and then feel guilty and even more depressed and inhibited. Obviously, assertiveness is an interpersonal style that has various social outcomes. Why are depressed clients not more assertive? It can be a basic skill deficit and this requires education in line with normal social skills training. However, there can also be a number of perceived disadvantages to becoming more assertive, most often loss of approval or abandonment. In some cases the lack of assertiveness has been the source of positive self-esteem (I am good because I'm not pushy). In fact, we can identify six basic themes that maintain a person in a submissive non-assertive state. The counsellor should explore the various reasons for inhibited assertiveness in depression. Below are listed some typical reasons.

*Fear of counter-attack* Here the person is fearful of being overwhelmed by the counter-response. There may be a fear they will become tongue-tied, mind go blank, look silly or forget what they want to say – the other will overpower them, be quicker etc. There can be a fear of loss of poise, or of asserting themselves badly and being subject to shame. We should also not forget that, more commonly than we would like to acknowledge, there can also be a fear of put-down or even injury by a more powerful other. Hence the basic fear is that they will come off the worst.

*Loss of control* Assertiveness can be physiologically arousing and some clients become fearful of this arousal in themselves. They may worry that they will lose control or say something extreme or shameful. Hence internal physiological cues can act as assertiveness inhibitors.

*Fear of abandonment* In these cases, clients fears that others will come to dislike them or abandon them if they are assertive. This normally applies to more intimate and friendship type relationships. Further, this is associated with ideas that they would not be able to cope alone, they would become worthless, unlovable or incapable.

*Rights* Some clients are unclear about their personal rights. They are apt to make various excuses for others' bad behaviour towards them or take the attitude 'Others are more important than me.' They feel guilt at putting themselves first or owning their own needs. They have a (superficially) over-caring attitude to others, but this is not always without a certain resentment that others do not (without them having to ask) recognize their needs. Although they allow themselves to be treated as doormats they would like others to respect them without having to assert themselves.

*Self-blame* It is not uncommon that clients blame themselves for conflict in some situations. Even women who are suffering from abuse at home may still blame themselves for it (Andrews and Brewin, 1990). Sometimes self-blame is a highly protective strategy for it reduces the chances of retaliation but it also increases depression, i.e. self-blame may inhibit their desire for revenge.

*Positive self and competitiveness*  Some clients suggest that they do not like assertive people and regard them as selfish. Hence they can feel good about themselves if they refrain from behaving like those 'selfish others'. In a way the lack of assertiveness is taken as evidence of a good self and a caring non-selfishness. To become more assertive threatens becoming similar to people they do not like, and losing a certain satisfaction with self that they are nicer than other people.

In any one case, each or all of these possibilities can be present. The client might also feel anger at what they see as other people's selfishness. They may have beliefs such as 'Others should not behave like that, they should know that it is wrong. I expect/demand people to behave as I think is right.' Clients might also have a wish for revenge. The advantages–disadvantages procedure usually reveals fairly quickly which themes are most problematic and counselling can be tailored accordingly. It can also be useful to role play situations such that clients can learn the behaviours associated with adaptive assertiveness and deal with negative cognitions that may arise. Often this is best handled in structured assertiveness groups. Many women who have been depressed attest to the benefits of these groups (see Dickson, 1982).

### Assertiveness, attractiveness and initiation

A particular problem with some depressed clients is that they do not initiate things that are positively reinforcing. In a factor analysis, Arrindell et al. (1988) found that assertiveness had at least four components: (a) display of negative feelings, involving standing up for oneself and engaging in conflict; (b) expression of and dealing with personal limitations, involving a readiness to admit mistakes and deficits; (c) initiating assertiveness, involving making one's opinion known; (d) praising others and accepting praise.

One of the clear findings from research is that depressed clients are not much fun to be with. This in part is because they do not initiate positive interactions. There are various reasons for this – shame, fear of rejection or attracting too much attention. Another reason may be high self-focused attention (e.g. see Pyszczynski and Greenberg, 1987). Resentment may also be important. For example, it is not uncommon to find that an individual does not initiate sex out of resentment towards the partner. Complying with sex, on the other hand, can give a sense of power and being needed. But initiation is an important social skill and our flow of positive social interaction depends on it. We could call this enthusiasm.

John was rather anxious about initiating social interactions. His wife found him difficult. He would sometimes sulk about the house and expect her to be sensitive and talk to him about what was on his mind (usually some minor grievance). If she made an enquiry, there would have to be a little ritual of denial that there was anything wrong followed by his wife insisting that there was. He would play the game of making her force it out of him. When his wife tired of this 'game' he became more resentful, attributing it to lack of care. Sulking can be quite a problem in some cases of depression (Dryden, 1992).

In sexual relationships it was a similar story. He would prefer his wife to initiate sexual contact and had to have clear signals that she desired sex. This again put a burden on his wife. Homework involved: (a) learning to give up the game of 'You have got to make me speak of my grievance as a test of your care'; (b) initiating at least one positive interaction per day; and (c) making his desire for sexual contact clear and 'up front'. For this John's wife was invited to counselling and he was surprised to learn how much she resented having to do all the emotional work.

Social explorative behaviour shows itself as taking interest in, and showing appreciation of, others. If one is initiating questions, ideas (or even sex) and generally exploring another person's view-point, then one is showing interest (see Heard and Lake, 1986, for discussion of the importance of this mutual, valuing interactional style). Being the recipient of interest is positively rewarding. It is not uncommon to find that rather passive individuals have histories of authoritarian parenting. A lack of socially explorative behaviour is unattractive, but too much initiation (e.g. sexual advances) and following one's own agendas/goals is also unattractive and is seen as dominating. Too much interest in another is intrusive. So it is a tricky balance and clients need to learn how to be sensitive to their partners, e.g. to accept a refusal of sexual contact gracefully without building up resentment or ideas like 'Right that's the last time I am going to make a pass at you.' These kinds of difficulty suggest a rather fragile sense of self.

It is, however, very common to find that significant others in the client's life are not valuing or appreciating of the client. It is common to find depressed clients (especially women) are living with emotionally neglectful or domineering partners. Interpersonal and evolutionary theory (Gilbert, 1992) suggests that we are not socially decontextualized beings, and all of us need at least some degree of positive signals of value from others. This is why social support comes out so strongly as a factor in both depression and recovery. Criticism by spouse is a predictor of relapse (Hooley and Teasdale, 1989).

Let us review the key issues in working with assertiveness problems.

---

Key issues 6.2  Assertiveness

1 Assertiveness is much more than just standing up for oneself in situations of conflict. It involves also positive initiations.
2 The counsellor can recognize that the client may have various fears of assertiveness (e.g. of the counter-attack or fear of rejection). These need to be made clear.
3 Lack of assertive behaviour often leads to resentment and this needs to be acknowledged.
4 Part of adaptive assertive behaviour is the ability to initiate positive behaviours and state clearly one's preferences. Sometimes depressed clients see this as selfish and think that they should do what others want.
5 Sulking can be a problem in depression and may be associated with fear of open assertive behaviour, and/or a sense of power that can be gained from withholding.
6 Counsellors may offer role play exercises to help clients explore their negative thoughts while enacting assertive roles.

---

### Rebellion

Jo was diagnosed as a chronic, mild depressive. He had seen a number of counsellors. He presented as a superficially pleasant and compliant client who appeared to do the homework agreed. On the surface he should have progressed well, but did not. In fact, he feigned agreement but had a passive aggressive style and was full of 'yes buts'. Previous counsellors had become frustrated with him. He could not understand why others eventually got angry or lost interest in helping him. Thus, our counselling focused early on issues of compliance. The counsellor noted that when Jo spoke of minor rebellions at school his eyes lit up and he become more 'emotionally expressive' during counselling.

The counsellor pointed this out. Could that spark be used to engage Jo? It was agreed that Jo should begin to argue during counselling why he should not do homework. It was agreed he would work on non-compliance. Once permission had been given for this 'rebellion', Jo took to counselling with vigour. The focus become his ability to resist others, including the counsellor.

> *Counsellor:* We agreed that you monitor some of your thoughts about doing jobs about the house. Is it likely that you will?
> *Jo:* [*with a slight smile*] I might, but knowing me I probably won't.

*Counsellor:* Good, so you will rebel. How does that feel?

*Jo:* [*pause, then cautiously*] I guess I feel a little bit stronger than you.

*Counsellor:* Is that okay or does that feeling worry you at all?

*Jo:* I know you say it is alright for me to rebel if I want to, but I think you will reject me if I go on like this. Sooner or later I am going to have to give in, aren't I, and work at counselling?

*Counsellor:* Hmm [*pause, watching Jo's nonverbal behaviour*] You look puzzled.

*Jo:* I can't believe you are encouraging me to rebel against this counselling. The other counsellors told me I had to work in the counselling or I wouldn't get better and you're telling me I don't have to.

*Counsellor:* It is not so much whether you work or not but how we work together. When you rebel we see you struggling to stay you. I would like to work with the rebel inside you not against it. Would you like to talk to the rebel inside?

After some discussion Jo agreed, just for the 'hell of it'. At this point we wrote on a card the typical thoughts the 'rebel' had. 'They can't make me do things. They will never get to me. They don't really understand – all smart arses every one.'

The tone of counselling at this point was like a game but, nevertheless, with the serious intent of eliciting basic beliefs and attitudes. Also, you will note that there were various envy elements in this theme. Jo was then encouraged to answer back at the schema. 'Okay, maybe others have put me down but aren't I cutting my nose to spite my face? I mean I might be able to resist others but that's not much fun in the end.' The counsellor also helped Jo to see the positive side of the rebel and talked openly that rebels had (sometimes) important uses, but they had to be part of the self and not running the whole show.

Whether Jo was convinced by 'the technique' or not, it changed his attitude to counselling. By validating the rebel and bringing it into sessions, he began gradually to be more open and hard working. Had the rebel in him not been acknowledged then counselling may have been difficult. Still this was a slow process. One could easily see how his more rebellious attitude would elicit anger in others and this in turn would reinforce his need to rebel, to hang on to his sense of self. His depression was of a passive–aggressive kind.

Much discussion focused on Jo's sense of strength and renewed vigour in being encouraged to rebel. Homework and other counselling procedures were seen as vehicles to help Jo internalize a stronger sense of self. Rebelling at counselling became 'Doing it my (his) way'. Slowly, Jo began to give up his pleasant but passive resistance and engage in more collaborative work. This case is cited to help counsellors see that one should try to work with their client's internal experience and not apply techniques because they seem logical or the correct way to do things. It is not unusual that openly helping clients rebel and become assertive is an important factor in change and here the counsellor may need to facilitate a certain degree of rebellion in the counselling which is safe and does not result in rejection.

Another area where it is very important to 'enable the rebel to speak' is in binge problems. Depressed clients who binge drink or binge eat are rarely doing it for comfort. Often the trigger is disappointment, frustration or the feeling of being put down or marginalized which is associated with rage. The thoughts associated with bingeing are 'Sod it, I've had enough. I'll show them. What do I care? They can't make me do XYZ. I'll make them feel bad – look what they made me do, etc.' At these times counsellors should be very cautious not to try to challenge by being punitive. Also, be sensitive to the shame that might follow when the patient is sober or out of the binge state. Try to be sensitive and not humiliate the client (unfortunately, a very common outcome). Rather, enable the client to verbalize their frustration and anger as the trigger, their desire to rebel and 'break out', to work out alternative behaviours for such anger, to recognize disappointment, and help the client recognize the rebel is working against them rather than for them.

## Concluding comments

This chapter has looked at various interpersonal themes and issues, and how the cognitive 'techniques' of chapter 4 can be integrated with an understanding of the client's interpersonal style. The self-experience remains a central focus but also concerns how the client acts in his or her social world. When using techniques, try to stay with the client's emotional experience and elicit affect where appropriate. It is particularly important to work with the fears (disadvantages) of changing. If clients are given the opportunity really to explore these fears and disadvantages, it is my experience that they move more easily through the process of change.

# 7

# Special Problems of Depressed Clients

## Shame

Shame has often been called the sleeper in psychopathology for it is often missed (Lewis, 1987a). Shame problems can result in important ideas and experiences going unexpressed. For example, adult survivors of child sexual abuse can go through counselling without the abuse being addressed (Jehu, 1988, personal communication). Shame can also produce powerful feelings of helplessness in both counsellor and client. Issues of 'stuckness' can sometimes hint at underlying shame. Some see shame as one of depression's primary associated affects (e.g. Mollon and Parry, 1984).

Much that passes in rational emotive counselling as shame is in fact embarrassment (Klass, 1990). Embarrassment overlaps with shame (both are concerned with self-presentation or 'how one lives in the mind of another'; Gilbert, 1992). But embarrassment is a much less severe affect. Hence shame-attacking exercises which involve acting in mildly embarrassing ways (e.g. speaking to a stranger as if they were a friend, or going to town with one's hair in a mess or dressed untidily) are inappropriate in severe depressive-shame. In this section we focus more on the issue of the experience of severe shame in the counselling relationship. In all cases, whether shame is mild or severe, empathic responses to the shame experience, efforts to raise self-esteem and stop self-downing remain key elements in the treatment.

The typical self–other evaluations that are part of shame are useful to consider because in shame the counsellor can be put in the position of the 'shaming other', i.e. you might inadvertently activate it (see table 7.1). Hence the counsellor can be seen as a source of possible ridicule. Cognitions include 'If the counsellor found this out about me he would reject me or be disgusted by me.'

There seem to be two major social comparison concerns in shame. The first relates to dominance and power and is concerned with rank, that is, inferior–superior evaluations. The second is

Table 7.1   *Shame experiences*

| Self (unable) | Other (able) |
| --- | --- |
| Object of scorn, disgust, ridicule, humiliation | The source of scorn, contempt, ridicule, humiliation |
| Paralysed, helpless, passive, inhibited | Laughing, rejecting, active, uninhibited, free |
| Inferior, smaller, weaker | Superior, bigger, stronger |
| Involuntary body response, rage, blush, tears, gaze avoidance | Adult and in control |
| Functioning poorly, mind going blank, desire to hide, conceal | Functioning well but experiencing contempt |
| Self in focal awareness | Other in focal awareness |

concerned with a sense of belonging and being like others, thus using the comparison of same–different. Brewin and Furnham (1986) found that the evaluation that one's inner experiences may be different from others in a negative way inhibits clients from sharing experiences and gaining consensus validation. A clinical example might be the new mother who has fears or aggressive feelings towards her baby, but evaluates these as abnormal and bad, and thus does not confide them to other women or helpers. Hence, these experiences remain as a source of negative self-evaluation. When counsellors talk of offering information for normalization, shame is often the issue that is addressed, although few writers acknowledge this.

Shame motivates concealment but concealment inhibits the assimilation of negative information about this self and has physiological affects, especially inhibition (Pennebaker, 1988). Thus, shame can be a major reason why affective experiences are not integrated into adaptive cognitive-affective schemata. Various writers have also noted the shame–rage spiral (Lewis, 1987a; Nathanson, 1987; Schore, 1991). A similar idea is Dryden's (1989b) concept of complex inference chains (see chapter 3). Here the cognitions of being evaluated negatively activate anger or rage. Typical cognitions are 'I hate/fear the counsellor finding out this about me. If he discovers how bad I am then he will reject me.

This will confirm that I am a bad/unworthy person. But if he doesn't find out, then I can't overcome these problems. So I feel angry and let down by the counsellor who is not helping me.' Or there might be thoughts such as 'I feel rage in this situation but I know it is inappropriate therefore I must be bad.' Thus shame motivates the desire to conceal and hide from view but it is also associated with a sense of badness and powerlessness. Some clients have difficulty in revealing that which they find shameful yet also want to confide. They can become angry or withdrawn with the counsellor who does not pick up on shame and probe the experience, thus giving the opportunity to reveal. Typical here is the client who says 'I wanted to tell you but you had to ask me directly before I felt able to tell you.'

## Working with shame

A typical shame problem can be in revealing the intensity of internal feelings. Mary found it extremely difficult to cry in counselling. When she did so she would cover her face with both hands and push back her tears. It was difficult to work with emotional material because she was deeply shame-prone. The focus in the early counselling was one of listening and trying not to engage her shame too quickly, on the assumption that before an empathic relationship had developed she might find it overwhelming and avoid counselling altogether. Gradually, however, the counsellor felt able to draw attention to the shame aspect.

> *Counsellor:* I note that you try to push back your tears at times.
> *Mary:* [*slightly angrily*] I have cried so much I don't want to cry here.

Because of the affects generated in previous sessions, I felt if I drew further attention to it I might be almost persecuting her in some way. Also I felt pushed out from her pain. This countertransference persecutory feeling in the counsellor is not uncommon in severe shame cases.

> *Counsellor:* [*gently*] Could we think about that a moment. What would crying here mean to you; I mean really letting go?
> *Mary:* I would feel vulnerable and exposed. It's a stupid thing to do and doesn't do any good.
> *Counsellor:* Stupid?

The fear of revealing powerful feelings is a common problem in some depressions and can say much about the internal self-structure and self–other schema. Many questions arise in the counsellor's mind at this point. Has the person been punished in the past for showing strong feelings of distress? In Mary's case the answer was almost certainly yes. Is the person angry with herself for having such feelings and is she trying to deny them? Does crying make her feel small/inferior in the eyes of the counsellor and in her own eyes?

From a technique point of view the counsellor tries to explore the disadvantages of crying and letting go of feelings; that is, the meaning of sharing feelings, but in a less structured way than discussed earlier. Here the counsellor has a choice of focus: (a) to reflect 'doesn't do any good'; or (b) the issue of vulnerability and exposure. If the former is chosen the discussion might become intellectualized. Alternatively, it might lead to discussion of previous experiences of being rejected. Hence, when a client gives two messages like this, the counsellor uses his/her judgement as to which aspect to focus on. 'Stupid' felt like a more self-evaluative concern and therefore this was the choice for reflection.

> *Mary:* [*crying*] I can't stand to feel like this.
> *Counsellor:* Because you feel exposed?
> *Mary:* [*nods*]
> *Counsellor:* Could you say more about feeling exposed?

This enables the client to talk more about the feelings and attitudes to crying rather than going into what the tears may be about and is therefore (possibly) less threatening.

> *Mary:* [*silence and then*] I feel it is somehow a weakness.
> *Counsellor:* [*gently*] Why are tears and distress a weakness?
> *Mary:* Because others can hurt you if they know your weakness. They might appear concerned but inside you know they are thinking you are pathetic.

Here Mary articulates basic mistrust of others and how they would respond to her distress. She cannot trust empathy responses from others, even if they are given. Does this apply to the therapeutic relationship? If it does it will make her ability to deal with high levels of distress very difficult. So we need to check this out.

> *Counsellor:* Would that be the same here, like I might see you as pathetic?
> *Mary:* I don't know. [*Looks up and sideways*] Why wouldn't you? You must get lots of stupid females bawling their eyes out.

Here the client reveals a desire not to be like those 'other bawling females', not to appear weak and stupid. How can the counsellor help here? Because the session has been moving to the discussion of emotionally painful material, emotion is activated in both counsellor and client. Can the counsellor contain it and not get defensive or feel persecutory? At this point, containment is just about staying with Mary and not pushing too hard. At the same

time the counsellor wants to try to convey a recognition of pain
and inner conflict and, if possible, focus on the underlying negative
self-evaluation. I know Mary has difficulties coping with the feelings of shame, that is crying in front of the counsellor, because she
has told me that she can and does cry on her own. There also
appears to be an increasing emergence of a rage–shame spiral (e.g.
her somewhat aggressive statement of 'Why wouldn't you?')

> *Counsellor:* [*gently*] I sense these painful feelings have been with you
> for a long time and they are deeply powerful for you. Maybe you are
> beginning to explore and understand them a little. Do they remind
> you of anything?
>
> *Mary:* [*beginning to cry more openly but also angry*] My father used to
> tease me if I cried. He'd call me poor little baby face or cry baby.
> I hated him for that. I really hated him. Nobody seemed to care why
> I cried and I just couldn't do anything.

Linking with the past had opened the opportunity to direct attention away from the present, and focus on painful memories.

> *Counsellor:* Hmm, so it is horrible when people don't recognize your
> feelings and put you down. That feels a very lonely place to be.
> [*Pause, then gently*] Mary, these feelings are painful to you because
> maybe you have never been able to share them before. But you are
> a human being and can feel hurt, deep hurt, and that doesn't make
> you weak, it makes you a feeling human being.

Here the counsellor has tried to empathize with her experience and
gives her a positive construction of feelings – being a feeling
human being. It is an attempt to rescue the self from internal
attack and rage. More important, the counsellor truly believes this
and it is not said 'matter of fact'. Mary was able to listen to this
intervention and after a long pause of quiet crying with hands over
her face said:

> *Mary:* I guess you are the only person that thinks so. [*Looks at the
> counsellor*] I think most of the time I hold back on feelings. Some
> think I'm cold maybe but I'm not. I just find it hard to show my feel-
> ings. It wasn't done in our family.

Mary then went on to talk in more depth about her family experience, as the counsellor quietly listened. A history of emotional
neglect began to come through. Here the affect remained high but
not overwhelming. At the end of the session the counsellor
repeated the positive statement of feelings.

> *Counsellor:* Well, Mary, given what you have said it is more than
> understandable why you have difficulty showing your feelings and yet
> in your heart you do feel things intensely. Perhaps as we work

together we can see this and help you reclaim those emotional bits that you had to bury.

*Mary:* [*softly*] Yes, I've done a lot of burying of things.

This is a recognition of her experience of hiding, concealing or splitting off, even from herself. Such an acknowledgement is an important change.

*Counsellor:* And this was because you viewed them as bad and weak. You have labelled yourself bad when you have strong feelings. Almost like your father did. Also you did not want to be in a position where you could be hurt or feel small.

*Mary:* Yes, that is how it has been.

*Counsellor:* Do you think it is time for you to have another look at this? Perhaps as a child burying feelings was self-protective and helpful. But things can be different now.

Here the counsellor points to the fact that at one time her coping behaviour may have been adaptive and again is not a sign of weakness or stupidity (see chapter 4).

*Mary:* Hmm.

*Counsellor:* So the first person to focus on is you and how you down yourself when you think about having strong feelings.

Deep shame is never easy to work with. Sometimes it lies behind emotional avoidance noted by clients' statements 'it's too painful to think about', although not all emotional avoidance is shame-based. So we can only offer a few guidelines. First, shame clients can stir up various feelings in the counsellor as a result of their need to conceal and especially if this is associated with rage. Clients can have a certain prickliness about them. However, the counsellor needs clearly to recognize these as part of the shame experience and think about the rage, loneliness and the fear of rejection that goes with the shame experience. Second, the counsellor needs to convey to the client that he/she senses and is trying to understand the struggle and the risk which the client feels is great. Third, the counsellor tries to make contact with the loneliness and emptiness of the client. If the therapeutic relationship is good, the recognition of loneliness can form a bridge to the shame issue. Finally, the counsellor is aware of the self-dislike and self-blame that are part of shame and these will be a source of work later in counselling. However, these points are only guides and there is much in this case that could take us through many chapters.

## Schema change in shame
Once the counsellor and client have set up a good working alliance

on shame (the client understands it and knows that the counsellor understands what happens in shame), it may then become possible to engage some shame-reducing work. Here the two chairs technique can be helpful. For example, for Mary we were able to elicit an internal dialogue and inference chain that went like this:

You should control your feelings.
It's weak to cry, bad to feel rage.
Paul will think you are pathetic.
You are pathetic when you cry.

Gradually, Mary began to identify how paralysed she felt under this kind of attack; how this was the same feeling she had as a child and became able to verbalize her feelings of helplessness and anger at this internal experience. She practised arguing with her father in role play. It was also possible to write some flash cards that she felt helped to challenge her feelings.

Crying is a sign of hurt not weakness.
If friends cry I would try to offer them comfort.
I can learn to work with my pain rather than hiding from it.
I have never allowed myself to cry without also attacking myself so I don't yet know if crying and caring for myself will be healing for me.
My father told me not to cry but I don't have to treat myself like he treated me.
What evidence do I have that Paul is likely to think like my father?

Another technique we used employed imagery. When Mary was in touch with some of her feelings of shame coming from early childhood, she imagined herself as the child coming into the counselling room saying 'Dad has been horrible to me.' Mary imagined herself putting her arm around the child and comforting her. In this way she was able to begin to activate a more nurturant mentality to herself (Gilbert, 1989). Of course, this was only an aspect of the work on her difficulties but it provided for a more self-accepting attitude to herself and allowed us to work on very emotional material. Slowly, she found that as she was able to express her feelings in the counselling she cried less on her own. Over the year in counselling, the rather depressed, brittle, angry and at times silent woman who came through the door on her first day softened.

Yet another possibility that we could have explored would have been the current schema, contributing life experiences and alternative constructions. All these approaches help in that they enable the person to be more focused on their internal meaning. Having things written down gives a focus and clarity to internal meaning-making processes and also helps to distance from the experiences. It may also be that this kind of repetition of the meaning of shame works as a kind of desensitization.

### The black hole of shame

In some cases of shame a client may fall into a state that can be described as a 'black hole'. For example, Jane had serious shame about her physical appearance, especially the shape of her body. This was an issue she wanted to discuss but each time we approached it her mind went blank and she began to feel highly scrutinized by the counsellor and very aware of being looked at. So overwhelming was this feeling that she felt paralysed. Her head would go down and she simply could not speak, while her main impulse was to run from the room. Ideas rushed through her mind, few of which she could focus on. These are intense states of inhibition.

This difficulty in verbalizing feelings might, by some counsellors, be seen as a problem of very early schema of the self which formed before language, thus making articulation of feeling difficult. However, it is equally possible that it results from high levels of internal inhibition (Gilbert, 1992). Counsellors sometimes wonder whether it is helpful to speak or remain silent in these situations. In my view the counsellor has to use empathic awareness to decide if a client is gradually working out of the state of inhibition or whether they are lost in it. In the latter case, the counsellor may need to do the work, for sometimes these states are not easy to get out of and sitting waiting for the client to speak tends to push the silence into an unhelpful position. Equally, going too quickly after self-evaluations can miss contact with the internal experience and the client simply switches off.

With these kinds of problem the counsellor can separate the first from subsequent occasions. Sometimes one can be taken by surprise when the black hole appears. Here the counsellor walks a difficult line between helping the client out of the black hole, and yet not interfering in a potentially important self-helping or self-recovery process. The empathic response can be helpful when it first appears.

Jane had sat in her chair for a long time unable to respond to the counsellor, trying to cut him out.

> *Counsellor:* This feels like a very painful state for you, Jane, especially with me sitting here looking at you. Maybe you are frightened of what I'm thinking.
> *Jane:* [*makes a slight head movement and half shrug*].

*Counsellor: [softly]* Okay, Jane. Now I am going to talk to you a little. What I am thinking is that you are in a lot of pain right now. Perhaps you have different emotions of anger, fear, loneliness, feeling cut off. I would like to help you out of that position. But maybe first it would be helpful if you had a better idea of what is going on in your mind and why. Would you allow me to try to explain some things about what we call shame and see if this helps?

*Jane: [nods]*.

*Counsellor:* Like I said, we call this a deep shame experience. They can come for all kinds of reasons but often because people have put us down in the past, and we can become unable to accept or like ourselves. When this comes over us we can have all kinds of feelings. We may wish to run away, or feel anger at ourselves and others, even the counsellor for being here.

Knowledge of shame is sometimes helpful because the person can see that it is a symptom of pain and fear and not a specific abnormality about them; they are not stupid or weak etc. After discussion of the shame experience, the client and counsellor may then discuss how they should act together if this state re-emerges in counselling. This is designed to help the client have more understanding and control in these situations. Thus some clients can indicate to the counsellor that they feel they are falling into the black hole and then the coping options worked out between them can be put into place. One client said 'It's been a great help knowing you understand my feelings and helping me understand what happens to me. I never realized what was happening. It just took me over.'

When severe shame feelings do arise, on later occasions, the counsellor might say something like 'Your feelings are trying to stop you from speaking. They are trying to protect you from ridicule and hurt perhaps. However, as we talked before you can say to these feelings "Thank you for your concern but I do not need your protection. I can gradually begin to explore these things now." If you think the black hole is getting too dark just stop for a moment, let's take stock and relax ourselves.'

In a sense this is a form of desensitization to the affects of deep shame via gradual exposure. Thus one is enabling a client to be less paralysed or overwhelmed by shame. Sooner or later, however, the client will need to talk about what it is they feel ashamed about. Fears may include previous sexual abuse, an abortion, homosexual feelings, aggressive feelings to children or to the counsellor, and so forth. If there is a good therapeutic relationship then usually the client has a wish to reveal and the counsellor can use this.

> *Counsellor:* I might be wrong about this but I sense there is something that you would like to discuss but are frightened to. Now I don't want to push you or anything, I just want you to know that this is how it seems to me.

Silence and other nonverbal signals to this statement usually suggest to the counsellor that he/she is on the right lines. Often the client will agree and then it is possible to explore further, but sometimes clients remain silent. The counsellor may then ask about fears of revealing, e.g. confidentiality or counsellor rejection. Just enabling the client to talk around the issue is helpful, but again this should not be undertaken without a good therapeutic relationship.

> *Counsellor:* I sense that there is a great risk for you, but we don't have to explore it all in one go. Is there some aspect of it that you could discuss and share here?

If sexual abuse is suspected the counsellor might say:

> *Counsellor:* You know, sometimes when we are young, people we trust do things to us that we sense is wrong or leaves us feeling ashamed. Maybe they interfere with us in some way. Has anything like that happened to you?

By careful and sensitive questioning that conveys an empathic awareness of the risks, the client can be helped to feel safe enough to reveal. Jehu (1988, 1989) has indicated how the cognitive approach can be used in cases of abuse. Family members in abuse cases may have used shame-invoking to inhibit the child from revealing to others, including telling the child that it was her fault or even denying that it happened at all. In one case the mother had not only denied the abuse, but had accused her daughter of being disgusting/terrible even to think that her father could have done such a thing. The experience of being disbelieved can be a powerful inhibitor of sharing feelings in counselling and is associated with feelings of guilt in revealing, and also disgust at self (Gilbert, 1992).

Let us now review some of the key issues in working with shame.

---

Key issues 7.1   Shame

1   Shame is about seeing oneself as inferior or bad in some way. Thus self-evaluation and negative self-experience are critical.
2   Shame motivates concealment and hiding.
3   Many of the affects of shame happen involuntarily and are difficult to control. Thus, even if a person wishes to reveal,

they might feel constrained from doing so (e.g. mind going blank, feeling paralysed and observed).

4 The counsellor can bring attention to the pain and fear of revealing (related to various beliefs and expectancies) and respond empathically to the patient's feeling state.

5 The counsellor starts a dialogue allowing the client to explore the shame experience but at the client's own pace. Sometimes clients will talk of having 'built up' to working on the shame problem.

## Guilt

Guilt is often confused with shame, but shame and guilt can be conceptualized as very different psychological processes (see table 7.2). Guilt often runs with shame since one's guilty behaviour might become known to another thus making one an object of rejection, scorn and put-down. However, guilt problems are often linked with thoughts and ideas about rights and entitlements (Gilbert, 1989). Guilt usually involves ideas of 'I should not want this' (e.g. an affair, more food) or 'I should not have done this.' Guilt as a 'should not' attitude often relates to moral dilemmas. There are, however, two main types of guilt:

1 Guilt about breaking one's own standards when these actions have little to do with other people (e.g. breaking a diet regime, spending money on oneself, having fantasies that break moral codes).

2 Guilt about actions that affect other people which break down into acts of commission and acts of omission. Acts of commission are doing things that hurt another, e.g. having an affair with a married person, hitting children etc. Acts of omission are things that one feels one could have done to be helpful, but did not do. Not caring enough is a common guilt scenario.

Strong guilt feelings often act as entrapments. For example, the person who stays in a marriage out of guilt may feel trapped in it yet also resentful and hopeless. At the same time they may feel needed which gives them some sense of self-esteem and power. Dickson (1982) calls this the compassion trap, and for individuals who have assertive problems associated with guilt, Dickson's book can be recommended reading on many counts. Guilt is often associated with basic beliefs such as 'I must put others first or I am a bad, selfish, unlovable person.'

Table 7.2  *Guilt experiences*

| Self (able) | Other (unable) |
| --- | --- |
| The source of hurt, let down or failure | Injured, needful, hurt |
| Intact and capable | Incapable, needing |
| Focus on self-actions and behaviours/feelings | Focus on let down/injury from other and own needs/losses |
| Efforts to repair | Efforts to elicit reparation or rejection/contempt, leading to shame |

Adapted from Lewis, 1986.
Self-blame does not distinguish shame from guilt but the power relationship does.

### Working with guilt

Doris' father came to live with her when her mother died. At first Doris was pleased to be able to help, but weeks turned to months and there was no sign that father was making plans to get his own place. Also he gave her little money to cover his living expenses and she felt that she could not ask him for more because it was his 'pension'. Doris tried to make hints that father should move but he turned things around by saying 'When you were in need we looked after you. I don't think I can cope on my own at the moment. Of course, if ever I thought you didn't want me any more then I would go.' His own guilt feelings were turned into attacks or claims of helplessness. Thus Doris felt helpless to confront her father because she thought this would make her a bad person.

In working with guilt, the counsellor tries to indicate the self-blame and issue of rights in a relationship while acknowledging the dilemmas. As Dickson (1982) points out, relating out of guilt can reduce the possible pleasures in the relationship. In mothers with young children, too much caring guilt can inhibit the pleasure of children, especially if these are associated with high standards in an effort to hold the title 'good mother'. Open discussion around these issues and efforts to share experiences with other mothers can be helpful in reducing guilt but from a cognitive point of view it is the self-labelling that is an important source of focus.

Sometimes caring guilt can arise from what Bowlby (1980) has called 'defensive exclusion'. Here the parents have instructed the child that any punishment or withdrawal of love is due to the child's bad behaviour and not their own. Thus children are educated not to blame their parents for their unreasonableness. The effect is to put the other (parent) beyond rebuke, and to exclude defensively their unreasonable behaviour. Hence some people come to counselling with little insight into their rights or entitlements, and are fearful of handing back responsibility to others who make unreasonable requests.

This links in with cultural values. For example, for obvious financial reasons the government of the past ten years has encouraged people to care for their elderly parents. The fact that people now live much longer than they did a few hundred years ago (thanks to modern medicine) is not acknowledged. Some feel guilty at not wishing to carry this burden. Thus, cultures vary in terms of their guilt- and shame-inducing tactics (Murphy, 1978). Feminists have pointed out that women have been so indoctrinated in the caring-loving role that guilt is a common problem. Let us review our thoughts about guilt.

---

Key issues 7.2  Guilt

1 Guilt in depression is often about trying to be good.
2 What type of guilt does the person suffer: (a) about the self; (b) about acts of commission or omission?
3 Look for the self-evaluation in guilt.
4 Look for the shoulds, should nots, and the musts in beliefs and attitudes.
5 Guilt can be a trap and lead to resentment, e.g. the compassion trap.
6 Explore cultural or social values that are maintaining guilt and discuss these with the client.

---

**Ideals**

Ideals are often powerful in depression, and often unrealistic (Moretti et al., 1990). Humans are future orientated. They plan with hopes, expectations and ideals related to positive outcomes. Our ideals involve a kind of matching to some internal standard, fantasy or template and can be the source of our shoulds, oughts and musts. They provide the source of information for how we would like things to be. They are the focus of various dysfunctional attitudes. Thus we are talking about a cluster of experiences that include ideals, aspirations, hopes and internal attitudes. We can have various types of ideals:

1 Ideals about how others should be, that is, our friends, lovers, spouse (e.g. understanding, fun, loving, accepting).
2 Ideals about how we should be (e.g. able, strong, anxiety free, competent, respected).
3 Ideals about how we should experience the world (e.g. fun, open, helpful).

Bibring (1953) based his early ego analytic theory of depression on the notion of ideals. Bibring suggested three types of ideals and aspirations which the (pre)depressive may seek:

1 The wish to be worthy and loved, and to avoid inferiority and unworthiness.
2 The wish to be strong, superior, secure, and to avoid being weak and insecure.
3 The wish to be loving and good and not aggressive, hateful or destructive.

In the last case, Bibring suggests that the awareness of internal aggressive impulses deals a blow to self-esteem. Bibring suggests that 'depression can be defined as the emotional correlate of a partial or complete collapse of the self-esteem of the ego, since it feels unable to live up to its aspirations . . . while they are strongly maintained' (Bibring, 1953: 25–6).

Becker (1979) points out that vulnerability to depression according to this model has a number of causes. These include: 'constitutional intolerance of persistent frustration, severe and prolonged helplessness, and developmental deficiencies in skill acquisition. These deficiencies are enhanced by the ego ideals which tend to be high and rigidly adhered to by depressives' (Becker, 1979: 324). Abramson et al. (1989) have developed a theory of what they call hopelessness depression derived from the perceived failure to be able to reach goals, standards or ideals.

The problem with strong ideals is that they activate disappointment when outcomes or events fall too far below the ideal. Thus the old phrase 'Don't expect too much and you won't be disappointed.' The empathic response tunes into the experience of disappointment. Disappointment in itself need not be a problem if it does not activate self- or other-attacking, but for some this is exactly what happens.

*Working with ideals*

Ken was in his forties when I first saw him. He had been known to the psychiatric services for thirty years. When he was eight his parents moved to another part of the country. Although he felt he had been popular in his old school, things turned out differently in his new junior school. His accent marked him as different and he had trouble understanding the teachers. His elder brother (by five years), on the other hand, did well in his new senior school, quickly became integrated, went on school trips and played various sports for the school teams. Their adaptation could not have been more different. Ken developed panic attacks and had much time away from school and was eventually sent to a school for children with emotional difficulties. Here also he felt he did not fit in. A strong theme in his life was that of the outsider.

Ken had developed a strong fantasy that if someone could cure his anxiety then he would be able to be like others, especially more like his brother who was successful both socially and in business. He idealized the medical profession but also had great rage at the way he thought he had been treated by them. When he was referred he was having panic attacks at home and spending days in bed, and saying he would kill himself, it was all pointless. ECT was considered.

At first the counsellor listened to the story for Ken was too angry to start exploring his own attitudes and felt that no one had understood him. The panics were fairly classic and focused on fears of being unable to breathe and dying. These responded to basic cognitive behaviourial intervention of breathing control, hyperventilation, gradual exposure and re-education. He did so well in counselling that he bought a new car and went on a trip to the continent. But when he came back he went to bed, got depressed and became very angry.

The problem was formulated as a problem of unrealistic ideals. Ken had the fantasy that if his anxiety was cured he would become 'turbo charged' and would make up for many lost years. For many years he had developed a fantasy of what it would be like to be anxiety free and not an outsider. In this fantasy he would be like others, able to travel, able to be successful, and in his words 'rejoin the human race at last'. He imagined that normal people never suffered anxiety. Also he had a hope that there would be some magic answer that would take the anxiety away, and that 'Once good it should stay good.' At this session he explained his trip. He had suffered anxiety on the trip over but had kept this under control.

We drew out two boxes that captured this situation. Ideal me = me without anxiety. Actual me = how I am now.

|  *Ideal me*  |  *Actual me*  |
|---|---|
| Like others | Not like others/different |
| Able to enjoy life | Life is miserable |
| Confident/successful | A failure |
| Explorative | Frightened |

*Counsellor:* As we have been talking it seems like you did quite a lot on your trip, but you feel disappointed with it. What happened when you got back?

*Ken:* I started to look back on it and thought, 'Why does it have to be so hard for me, always fighting this anxiety?' I should have enjoyed it more after all the effort I put into it. I should have done more. It's been a struggle. So I just went to bed and brooded on how bad it all was and what's the point.

*Counsellor:* From what we have discussed before it sounds like your experience did not match your ideal.

*Ken:* Oh yeah, it was far from that.

*Counsellor:* Okay, what went through your mind when you found that the trip was not matching your ideal.

*Ken:* I started to think I should be enjoying this more. If I were really better I would enjoy it more. If I felt better I would do more. I'll never get on top of this. It's all too late and too much effort.

*Counsellor:* That sounds like it was very disappointing to you.

*Ken:* Oh yes, very, terribly, but more so when I got back.

*Counsellor:* What did you say about you?

*Ken:* I've failed again. I just felt totally useless. After all the work we've done nothing has changed.

*Counsellor:* Let's go back to our two boxes for a moment and see if I have understood this. For many years you've had the fantasy of how things would be if you were better [*points to ideal box*]. But getting there is a struggle and this is disappointing to you. When you get disappointed you start to attack yourself saying that you are a failure and it's too late. That makes the actual you seem unchanged. Is that right?

*Ken:* Yes, absolutely.

*Counsellor:* Can we see how the disappointment of not reaching the ideal starts up this internal attack on yourself, and the more of a failure you feel the more anxious and depressed you get?

*Ken:* Hmm, yes.

In Ken's case we were able to work with the link joining the ideal, the disappointment and the self-attack. Later in the session we were able to explore the successes that had taken place on the trip and explore how Ken would disqualify the positive if it did not match up to an ideal. He saw it as 'destroying and ripping up the good things that happened to him'.

There were other issues such as the new self-schema of being able to travel and no longer being a victim to anxiety. His new sense of self was 'strange' to him and he worried that if he became well others would not be so interested in helping him. However, slowly Ken began to modify his ideal and gradually mourn lost opportunities. But this took a long time and counselling lasted well over a year.

So shoulds often point to ideals. The self-attacks come from the disappointment and this makes the person feel further away from the ideal. Unfortunately, these attacks, consequent to disappointment, and the failure of others to fulfil various needs for the client, can fuel aggression also. In one case a young man had very unrealistic fantasies of how a loving relationship would be (and was highly egocentric). When his lovers did not live up to his ideal image, he expressed his disappointment in violence. He had a lot of difficulty in giving up the ideal ('they should be . . .' thoughts) as his needs for constant attention were great.

Thus, counselling explores the shoulds, oughts and musts implicit in high ideals. It is helpful to be aware of the experience of disappointment that is consequent upon failing to reach high ideals. Type A personalities can also have difficulty in changing their standards because this may mean that they will not be able to get to their ideal of being more special or superior to others. In these cases the advantages–disadvantages of changing ideals can be helpful. Thus in counselling a certain working through of disappointment is often necessary.

---

Key issues 7.3   Ideals

1 Ideals represent our hopes and aspirations of how we would like things to be. These can be drawn out by the counsellor with questions: 'how would you like it to be, how would you like yourself to be . . .?'

2 Depressed clients can have unrealistic ideals and feel a strong sense of disappointment when ideals are not achieved.

3 In cognitive approaches ideals may lead to depression if a person says to themselves 'I must have my ideal or I am bad and weak. If I cannot reach/have my ideal it is pointless.'

4 At times, depressed patients are so disappointed by failing to reach their ideals that they destroy the positive and engage in black–white thinking.

5 Helping clients recognize the thoughts and feelings that are triggered by the disappointment is a key to working with ideals.

## Envy

Envy, like shame, arises out of self–other comparisons, and where the person feels they are in some sense inferior. In competitive cultures which stress individualism, envy is unfortunately rife (Gilbert, 1989, 1992). There are various forms of envy.

*Fear of igniting other people's envious attacks*    In Ken's case, discussed above, some years before starting counselling he bought a new car but sold it three months later. When asked why, he said that while driving around he had the idea that others were looking at him thinking 'Where the hell did he get the money from to buy that? Who does he think he is?' Thus, Ken had an acute sense of external persecution. His family history revealed much envy as part of the family dynamics.

> *Counsellor:* Even if it is true that others would be envious of you, why would that mean you had to sell the car?
> *Ken:* I wouldn't want them to think like that. They would try to put me down.
> *Counsellor:* But suppose we said, look envy is part of life and we have to learn to cope with it rather than hide from that. What would you say?
> *Ken:* Hmm, I am not sure about that.
> *Counsellor:* Okay, let's look at the advantages and disadvantages of accepting other people's envy.

This revealed many advantages: 'I would be free to have what I want (cars, clothes, etc). I would feel more in control of my life, not having to look over my shoulder. I would feel better and more hopeful.' However, the disadvantages were many: 'Others would think I was above my station. They might try to hurt or pull me down. They will think I'm okay and don't need help. They wouldn't want to help if I needed it. They might take pleasure in seeing me fall. I might become even more of an outsider.'

> *Counsellor:* It sounds like you actually have a certain terror of success and changing.
> *Ken:* Written down like that I see it. I do get very anxious about what others think if good things happen to me.
> *Counsellor:* Yeah, but it's more than that, it's a belief that others will pull you down, won't help you and that you would not be able to cope with that.

Exploration of history had revealed a father figure who had rarely praised Ken, in part because he was never as good as his brother and in part because, while the brother was seen as advancing the family and giving it pride, the father had not taken that view of Ken. Thus, when Ken had bought this new car and proudly shown it to his father, his father had simply commented that he could not see the point of Ken having a car like that in his situation. Also, the father had seemed mildly angry that this son, who had been anxious and depressed all these years, should have a new car.

Much discussion was given over to these aspects with the counsellor acting in an encouraging way (or in self psychology terms, Wolf, 1988, a mirroring self object). Thus, one homework for Ken was to begin to look at new cars and eventually buy one, which he did. Also he discussed openly with friends about his feelings and many of them said 'Good luck mate, if you can afford it.' One of his friends said 'There's no pockets in shrouds' and this motto stuck. Thus, he sought out other sources of evidence. In some ways the fear of other people's envy can be seen as a form of need for approval. However, in envy it is not only disapproval that is feared but actual attacks, subsequent refusals of help and becoming isolated. In Ken's case there was a clear conflict between being seen as injured and needy and being successful and contented.

*Fear of one's own envy* Anne was depressed but also had thoughts of wanting to bring other people down. 'If only I can make them feel like I do, that would wipe the smile off their faces.' There were also various aggressive fantasies. However, these feelings made her feel more isolated and she took them as evidence of a bad, unlovable self (i.e. a source of shame).

> *Anne:* Until I got this depression, I never realized I could feel so vengeful. I see my friends having fun and I think I used to be like that. Why me? Why not them? I actually hate them for being happy. It's terrible. Perhaps I deserve this because inside I'm so nasty.
> *Counsellor:* So you have two issues. One is your vengeful feelings, and the other is that you see this as evidence of you being nasty?
> *Anne:* Yes. I hate to feel this burning resentment when I am with others.
> *Counsellor:* So your resentment makes you feel different, not like others?
> *Anne:* Oh yes, and so does my depression. I used to be like them. I rarely had time for depressed people. I know what they must be thinking about me now. But, of course, I try to hide it.

At this point Anne talked at length about the loss of her old self, and her anger at what had 'happened to her'. As we moved back to envy again, the counsellor tried to focus on the sequence of envy leading to negative self-beliefs, leading to loss of good happy-self.

*Counsellor:* Okay, let's think about envy for a moment. Suppose you could allow yourself to feel envy without saying this means you are nasty?

*Anne:* But it is nasty, Paul. It's so destructive. I don't want to feel this. I want to be well again.

*Counsellor:* Yes, that is our goal, but on the way we are trying to explore your negative ideas about yourself which right now focus on envy.

*Anne:* Hmm, I don't want to feel envy.

*Counsellor:* Well, let's draw it out.

The counsellor then draws a circle with the links: feel envy at being depressed, this means I'm nasty, feel worse about myself leading to more depression and more envious feelings.

*Counsellor:* You see, if we could work on the 'this means I'm nasty' that may help you feel less negative about yourself. It is a rather global judgement which gives you the feeling of a lost good self that you had previously.

*Anne:* If I'm not nasty then what am I?

*Counsellor:* Well, let's think about alternatives? In general, why are people envious – oh, apart from being nasty [*client smiles*]?

*Anne:* [*thinks*] Hmm, I guess they feel one down or in need like we said before.

*Counsellor:* Does that seem reasonable, that people can feel envy when inside they feel needing of something?

*Anne:* Yes, I think so.

*Counsellor:* So supposing we applied those judgements to you and said your envious feelings reflect a need to be well and like others again, rather than as evidence of a nasty self?

*Anne:* I'd have to think about this.

*Counsellor:* Fine, [*smiles*] let's think about it.

The counsellor then worked with changing the self-judgement such that the client began to reconsider envy in terms of feelings of need and being different from others and not as evidence of a nasty person. Envy became an unpleasant affect that was understandable rather than an internal experience that made her feel bad about herself. Gradually, as Anne began to accept her envy and other destructive feelings without attacking herself, she was able to talk more to her friends about her depression and gradually recovered. Later, she also revealed that my approach to her envy and my refusal to see it as evidence of her nastiness had helped her accept it and work it through.

---

Key issues 7.4   Envy

1 Envy relates to powerful feelings and beliefs about being different from others and less than others in some way.
2 Envious feelings themselves often increase the sense of difference and of being an outsider.
3 The counsellor helps the client accept his/her envy, and recognize that it is often related to some feelings and beliefs about need rather than evidence of a bad or nasty self.
4 In some depressions, experiences of envy can be destructive of counselling if they are not acknowledged. At times, a client might feel envious of the counsellor (or counsellor's life style) and has difficulty working in an alliance.

---

**Concluding comments**

In this chapter we have focused primarily on the way an internal experience can become one of internal self-attack. This lies at the heart of the cognitive approach (Beck, 1967; Beck et al., 1979). Most automatic thoughts associated with depression are (negatively) self-evaluative. What we have explored here is that these self-evaluative aspects are often focused on self–other comparisons with various fears of rejection and put-down. Counsellors can learn to empathize with these feelings and attitudes and be more aware of them. Also, counsellors can learn how to avoid activating resistance by themselves behaving in a shaming, critical and patronizing manner. In depression, shame, guilt, ideals and envy are of special importance.

# 8

# Termination and Personal Reflections on Depression

Termination of counselling with the depressed client follows some general principles (Ward, 1989). These general points can be relevant not only to the ending phase but throughout counselling.

*Normal sadness* In any relationship where there has been emotional sharing, support and encouragement, there can be sadness and reluctance at saying goodbye. The counsellor may be the first person with whom the client has shared certain aspects of their lives, and their deeper thoughts.

*Reactivating schemata* An approaching termination can be a time when the client may re-experience, in a mild way, fears of abandonment or coping alone. These can be addressed, not in order to prolong counselling, but to give new opportunities to work with the affects and beliefs of leaving and separating.

*Termination as a process* Preparing to leave is a process not a sudden cessation of counselling and therefore needs to be discussed before it actually occurs. Ending is a stage in a process and is planned for (Egan, 1990). The client's thoughts and feelings about 'life beyond counselling' are explored. In some, short-term therapies, termination is an issue discussed right from the start as the counsellor negotiates the number of sessions.

*Follow up* With many depressed clients it may be appropriate gradually to space the counselling sessions; for example, moving from (say) weekly to fortnightly to monthly and then to a six-month follow up. Many clients have chronic problems or have had severe episodes and it is inappropriate to terminate without this gradual process. Some depressed clients show what is called 'a flight in health' but can relapse subsequently. This kind of gradual tailoring off may help avoid sudden relapses. It also allows the client to move from an intense working relationship to a less intense working relationship. Clients benefit from having the opportunity for a general review at some point distant to the intense period. Frank et al. (1989) compared drug treatment and interpersonal counselling for depression, and found that interpersonal counselling (only once a month) was the best predictor of length of interval to a relapse, i.e. the clients receiving it stayed well longer.

*Booster sessions*   A counsellor can negotiate with the client the possibility of booster sessions. These may be either on an 'if and when' basis or planned into a follow up. One needs to be aware of cultural attitudes towards independence which can result in ideas that once a client has left counselling they should never need help again. However, it is wise to make clear that booster sessions are not the same as re-entering counselling, and usually they are only one or a few in number. Of course, if a client has had a major relapse into depression then re-entering counselling may be appropriate, along with considerations of other treatment possibilities.

*The counsellor's attitude to termination*   Both counsellor and client can have separation work to do. For example, during my own training, I found that addressing the issue of termination was difficult and I had to work through my own thoughts and feelings at addressing this with clients. To some degree I had a problem with a hidden paternalistic attitude and caring guilt.

*Unrealistic ideals*   Another aspect I had to face was that I had unrealistic ideals about what the counselling could/should achieve. I had beliefs like 'People should be happy ever after.' I am very grateful for my supervision for helping me with this. Clients too can have unrealistic ideals of what 'being well' means. Thus, as indicated earlier, the counsellor and the client should discuss the aims and expectations of the counselling enterprise. Also clients and counsellors should be aware that in a sense one never stops the process. Self-monitoring, and refusing to self-attack, to treat self and others with compassion and respect, are all things that one continues to struggle with throughout life.

*Questions about termination*
There are certain obvious questions about termination. These include: (a) does the client feel better; (b) has he/she changed in the styles of thinking and relating; (c) has his/her self-esteem increased; (d) can he/she cope better with major life events, and

so forth (Ward, 1989; Egan, 1990). However, termination might also arise from more negative influences, e.g. family are resistant to the client's attendance, financial or time constraints, problems and pressure of working with long-term cases in the National Health Service, poor relationship with the counsellor, feelings/beliefs of not getting anywhere. Negative client attitudes might include beliefs of being a burden (e.g. thinking that there are other clients who need the counsellor more). These issues need to be addressed openly and, if possible, ways to cope with them negotiated.

Premature termination is normally defined as occurring when a client has an appointment but, without notice, does not attend further. In my practice, I normally try to contact the client and discuss his/her reasons for non-attendance, not (obviously) in an accusing way but to explore with the client potential difficulties. If a client is very depressed, is drinking heavily or may be a suicide risk, then other agencies need to be contacted (e.g. the general practitioner). Where possible, I leave it open for clients to attend while at the same time respecting their wishes. One has to make the balance between caring for the conflicts of the client in attending, yet without being coercive. I have the impression that contacting clients is helpful. However, the psychology of this may be different in a free system like the British National Health Service from an American or private service where people have to pay. Sometimes shame is a factor in non-attendance. On the telephone the client may verbalize cognitions such as (a) it's been a terrible week and I thought you'd get fed up with me; (b) I just couldn't face you after what we talked about last week; (c) I was too depressed to get out of bed and was too ashamed to call you; and even (d) I wanted to feel better before I saw you.

### Where to now?

Recent research on depression has shown that many types of intervention and counselling are effective. Beckham (1990) has written a major overview of research into the psychological treatment of depression. Findings suggest that many orientations, including psychoanalytic, cognitive, interpersonal and behavioural, show positive effects. Evidence suggests that the central variables are counsellor skill, client difficulty and characteristics of the dyadic interaction. Beckham also notes that it is difficult to make clear predictions of outcome because so many factors can be involved, e.g. possible biological dysfunctions, the importance of life events both as triggers of depression and (when positive) as recovery factors, and the quality of external support systems. For these reasons and others, I advocate the biopsychosocial approach (Gilbert, 1984, 1989, 1992).

Recently, concern has been expressed in the psychological literature that some depressions become 'over-psychologized' (Goudsmit and Gadd, 1991), and that important biological factors are missed. Also the counsellor should be aware that there are many different forms of counselling which have a different focus. It is possible that some depressed clients will benefit from other ways of working with other types of counsellor, even if they do not benefit from this particular approach (Karasu, 1990). (See also Corey, 1991, and Dryden, 1990, for excellent general overviews of different schools and models of counselling.)

Other factors to consider include premorbid functioning. First, to what extent is this depression the result of life events that have overloaded coping ability and produced a collapse of self-esteem? In these cases a client may respond rather quickly to counselling, pick up on the various techniques, and work towards health. However, a depression often reveals particular difficulties that have become embedded in a certain life style and interpersonal way of relating. There may also be a sense of revisiting something, that is the depression seems to reactivate early schemata with their associated affects. This is entirely consistent with Beck's (1976) notion of latent schemata and more recent interpersonal approaches (Safran and Segal, 1990). Hence counselling is something of a journey which includes development and maturational change. In this sense the counselling must adapt to the developmental abilities of the client (Katakis, 1989).

## Training and supervision

Counsellor skill is a factor that is related to outcome. Thus it is important that counsellors should have access to good training opportunities. Many of the skills outlined here are best learned under supervision. Second, counsellors working with depressed clients should be familiar with the different theories of depression (Gilbert, 1992). The role of personal counselling for the counsellor is a complex one, but many agree that some kind of personal experience is helpful (Dryden, 1991).

Counsellors should be aware of certain of their own cognitions that can make counselling difficult and also be a source of negative feelings. Some common, unhelpful counsellor beliefs are:

*Beliefs about technique*

1 If a client isn't getting better my technique is wrong.
2 To help clients improve I must get to my techniques quickly.
3 I don't know my techniques well enough, therefore I can't help clients.
4 I don't seem to know what is going on with this client therefore the counselling can't be helpful.
5 I must be able to help this person (or all clients) in order to regard myself as a good counsellor or even a good person.
6 If I can't help people then I am a no good person.
7 I must never feel anxious with a client (with heart rate going up etc).
8 I must like my clients.
9 I must never be moved to tears with a client.
10 I must never show a client I am confused and ask for clarity (i.e. I must cover my thoughts. Shame in the counsellor is an unacknowledged problem in my view).
11 I must constantly challenge clients.

*Beliefs about the client*

1 Empathy and being with a client is not enough; they have to do some work.
2 If the client can't understand the techniques (or work with them) they won't get better.
3 If clients can't articulate their thoughts they won't get better.
4 If clients don't change quickly they won't change at all.
5 This client likes being depressed.
6 Depressed people are basically weak people (a more common automatic thought than is acknowledged).
7 I could never get that depressed myself.
8 This client is manipulative.

And, finally, 'If I have any of the above beliefs I am a bad person. I shouldn't have these beliefs – the book says so.' Frankly, we all have automatic thoughts like these at times. But if we can stay open, check them out, allow them to come into our awareness, talk them over with a colleague, rather than turning a blind eye to them, then we can be more helpful to ourselves and our clients. In essence this is about being in tune with the counter-transference (Watkins, 1989b).

There are many other beliefs and one can make it a point of interest, rather than fear and dread, to try to find them. How many negative thoughts did you have in your work today? If you treat yourself with compassion and honesty and do not demand that you are always a perfectly nice counsellor with perfectly pure thoughts, then you may become less anxious or demoralized with depressed clients.

To be proficient and stay proficient, requires an open capacity to learn via reading, studying, taking refresher courses, and discussing with other counsellors (Dryden, 1991). The cognitive counsellor remains open and knows that at all times there is more to be learnt, that counselling itself is a process and if we find that at times we are stumped or lost or make mistakes we can take this as a challenge rather than as a self-rebuke. Never put your own self-evaluations on the line in counselling for this may lead to defensiveness and needs for the client to get better to prove to you how good you are. Kouholt and Rønnestad (1992) have recently published a fascinating study of how therapists change over time. Becoming less focused on a client's need to change is a major part of professional development. Some clients remain difficult despite our best efforts. You may not be able to help everyone that walks through your door. Some will require different types of intervention, and some clients with chronic difficulties tax all therapies of whatever type.

## Personal reflections

Most therapies for depression reflect theories of cause and/or maintaining factors. The theory that I endorse is derived from evolution theory. This (stated briefly) suggests that depression arises from loss of social power and inferiority. Most animals form dominance hierarchies and those at the bottom are biologically stressed, tend to be inhibited in their explorative behaviour and show similar (but not identical) biological patterns to depressed individuals. In humans, evaluations of self-esteem are related to status and how we feel others regard, value and treat us. It is inappropriate to spell this theory out here (see Gilbert, 1992) but to say simply that a positive sense of self is based on the signals of valuing we receive from others and give to ourselves (Brown and Harris, 1978, see esp. chs 15 and 16).

The purely cognitive view, that we are in some sense socially decontextualized beings who disturb ourselves only by our thoughts, seems to be theoretically flawed, not supported by the evidence, and politically dubious. In child-rearing we know that neglect and hostile parenting can have major effects on the developing nervous system, the maturational process and subsequent vulnerability to mental ill health. Further, these negative early effects can be difficult to overcome. Thus, for me, cognitive theory neglects the role of the environment (and the way an environment can be down-putting, critical, hostile, inhibiting and/or neglectful), places too much stress on the individual and is out of tune with evolutionary and biological theories of mind. We are highly social animals, and our internal mental mechanisms evolved to live a social life. Being put down and feeling oneself to be inferior are therefore key elements in depression. Nevertheless, although the *cognitive theory* of depression is suspect, helping clients take responsibility for their own thoughts, avoid internalizing hostility and recognize the nature of their own self-attacks, give up self-attacking and recognize patterns of thinking (e.g. personalization, shame cognitions, global evaluating, black–white thinking, unrealistic ideals etc.) is often a key to successful outcome.

It follows therefore that my main focus in treating depression is in the domain of inferiority and put-down (Gilbert, 1992). These may come from the environment in the form of hostile attacks, constant verbal put-downs from dominant others, or neglect and lack of interest. They can also come from within ourselves in the form of devaluing the self, self-attacking and seeing oneself as inferior and an outsider. Thus, for me, the core of treating depression is to focus on helping the client value (rather than devalue) themselves and their primary relationships. For me, depression is about social powerlessness. It is understandable, therefore, why various forms of counselling that increase a client's self-esteem by sending signals of valuing their experience (listening, respecting, encouraging, supporting, teaching, sharing, Frank, 1982) can be effective to some degree. The cognitive-interpersonal approach goes further in directly helping the client identify self-downing, and the way that they make unreasonable demands on themselves and, at times, others. All these work on the internal self-valuing system. Thus I endorse the cognitive model not because I believe that disorder arises from some kind of irrationality, but because there are mechanisms in the brain that respond in certain kinds of ways to certain kinds of input. One does not have to follow a rational/irrational model of mental disorder to be able to work as a cognitive counsellor (Mahoney and Gabriel, 1987).

I hope that what you find in this book will help your work with depressed clients, be responsive to their special problems, their low self-esteem, poor self-valuing, their self-attacks, their sense of disappointment, shame, guilt and envy. All these, I would suggest, are social cognitions with a focus on social power and control, and relative standing in relation to others.

# Bibliography

Abramson, L.Y., Metalsky, G.I. and Alloy, L.B. (1989) Hopelessness: A theory-based subtype of depression. *Psychological Review*, 96, 358–72.

Andrews, B. and Brewin, C.R. (1990) Attributions of blame for marital violence: A study of antecedents and consequences. *Journal of Family and Marriage*, 52, 757–67.

Argyle, M. (1984) *The Psychology of Interpersonal Behaviour*, 4th edn. Harmondsworth: Penguin.

Argyle, M. (1987) *The Psychology of Happiness*. London: Methuen.

Argyle, M. (1991) *Cooperation: The Basis of Sociability*. London: Routledge.

Arieti, S. and Bemporad, J. (1980a) The psychological organization of depression. *American Journal of Psychiatry*, 137, 1360–5.

Arieti, S. and Bemporad, J. (1980b) *Severe and Mild Depression: The Psychotherapeutic Approach*. London: Tavistock.

Arrindell, W.A., Sanderman, R., Van der Molen, H., Van der Ende, J. and Mersch, P.P. (1988) The structure of assertiveness: A confirmatory approach. *Behaviour Research and Therapy*, 26, 337–9.

Baker, H.S. and Baker, M.N. (1988) Arthur Miller's 'Death of a Salesman': Lessons for the self psychologist. In A. Goldberg (ed.), *Progress in Self Psychology*, vol. 4. Hillsdale, NJ: The Analytic Press.

Bandura, A. (1977) *Social Learning Theory*. Englewood Cliffs, NJ: Prentice-Hall.

Beach, S.R.H., Sandeen, E.E. and O'Leary, K.D. (1990) *Depression in Marriage*. New York: Guilford Press.

Bebbington, P., Katz, R., McGuffin, P., Tennant, C. and Hurry, J. (1989) The risk of minor depression before age 65: Results from a community survey. *Psychological Medicine*, 19, 393–400.

Beck, A.T. (1967) *Depression: Clinical, Experimental and Theoretical Aspects*. New York: Harper and Row.

Beck, A.T. (1976) *Cognitive Therapy and the Emotional Disorders*. New York: International Universities Press.

Beck, A.T. (1983) Cognitive therapy of depression: New perspectives. In P.J. Clayton and J.E. Barrett (eds), *Treatment of Depression: Old Controversies and New Approaches*. New York: Raven Press.

Beck, A.T. (1987) Cognitive models of depression. *Journal of Cognitive Psychotherapy: An International Quarterly*, 1, 5–38.

Beck, A.T., Emery, G. and Greenberg, R.L. (1985) *Anxiety Disorders and Phobias: A Cognitive Approach*. New York: Basic Books.

Beck, A.T., Epstein, N., Harrison, R.P. and Emery, G. (1983) Development of the sociotropy-autonomy scale: A measure of personality factors in depression. Philadelphia: University of Pennsylvania.

Beck, A.T., Freeman, A., and Associates. (1990) *Cognitive Therapy of Personality Disorders*. New York: Guilford Press.

Beck, A.T., Rush, A.J., Shaw, B.F. and Emery, G. (1979) *Cognitive Therapy of Depression*. New York: Wiley.

Becker, J. (1979) Vulnerable self-esteem as a predisposing factor in depressive disorders. In R.A. Depue (ed.), *The Psychobiology of the Depressive Disorders: Implications for the Effects of Stress*. New York: Academic Press.

Beckham, E.E. (1990) Psychotherapy of depression research at a crossroads: Directions for the 1990s. *Clinical Psychology Review*, 10, 207–28.

Belsher, G. and Costello, C.G. (1988) Relapse after recovery from unipolar depression: A critical review. *Psychological Bulletin*, 104, 84–6.

Berndt, D.J. (1990) Inventories and scales. In B.B. Wolman and G. Stricker (eds), *Depressive Disorders: Facts, Theories and Treatment Methods*. New York: Wiley.

Bibring, E. (1953) The mechanism of depression. In P. Greenacre (ed.), *Affective Disorders*. New York: International Universities Press.

Birtchnell, J. (1990) Interpersonal theory: Criticism, modification and elaboration. *Human Relations*, 43, 1183–201.

Blackburn, I.M. (1989) Severely depressed in-patients. In J. Scot, J.M.G. Williams and A.T. Beck (eds), *Cognitive Therapy in Clinical Practice*. London: Routledge.

Blackburn, I.M. and Davidson, K. (1990) *Cognitive Therapy for Depression and Anxiety*. Oxford: Blackwell.

Blatt, S.J., Quinlan, D.M., Chevron, E.S., McDonald, C. and Zuroff, D. (1982) Dependency and self criticism: Psychological dimensions of depression. *Journal of Consulting and Clinical Psychology*, 50, 113–24.

Book, H.E. (1988) Empathy: Misconceptions and misuses in psychotherapy. *American Journal of Psychiatry*, 145, 420–4.

Bowlby, J. (1973) *Separation, Anxiety and Anger. Attachment and Loss*, vol. 2. London: Hogarth Press.

Bowlby, J. (1980) *Loss: Sadness and Depression. Attachment and Loss*, vol. 3. London: Hogarth Press.

Boyd, J.H. and Weissman, M.M. (1981) Epidemiology of affective disorders. *Archives of General Psychiatry*, 38, 1039–46.

Brewin, C.R. (1988) *Cognitive Foundations of Clinical Psychology*. London: Lawrence Erlbaum Associates.

Brewin, C.R. and Furnham, A. (1986) Attributional and pre-attributional variables in self-esteem and depression: A comparison and test of learned helplessness theory. *Journal of Personality and Social Psychology*, 50, 1013–20.

Brown, G.W. (1989) Depression: A radical social perspective. In K. Herbst and E. Paykel (eds), *Depression: An Interactive Approach*. Oxford: Heinemann Medical Books.

Brown, G.W. and Harris, T. (1978) *The Social Origins of Depression*. London: Tavistock.

Burns, D.D. (1980) *Feeling Good*. New York: Morrow.

Clarkin, J.F., Haas, G.L. and Glick, I.D. (1988) *Affective Disorders and the Family: Assessment and Treatment*. New York: Guilford Press.

Collins, N.L. and Read, S.J. (1990) Adult attachment, working models, and relationship quality in dating couples. *Journal of Personality and Social Psychology*, 58, 644–63.

Corey, G. (1991) *Theory and Practice of Counselling and Psychotherapy*. California: Brooks/Cole.

Cox, J.L. (1988) The life event of child birth: Sociocultural aspects of postnatal depression. In R. Kumar and I.F. Brockington (eds), *Motherhood and Mental Illness*, vol. 2: *Causes and Consequences*. London: Wright.

Coyne, J.C. (1976a) Depression and response to others. *Journal of Abnormal Psychology*, 85, 186–93.

Coyne, J.C. (1976b) Towards an interactional description of depression. *Psychiatry*, 39, 28–40.

Coyne, J.C. (1982) A critique of cognitions as causal entities with particular reference to depression. *Cognitive Therapy and Research*, 6, 3–13.

Deitz, J. (1988) Self-psychological interventions for major depression. *American Journal of Psychotherapy*, XL11, 597–609.

Dickson, A. (1982) *A Woman in your own Right*, rev. edn. London: Quartet Books.

Driscoll, R. (1989) Self-condemnation: A conceptual framework for assessment and treatment. *Psychotherapy*, 26, 104–11.

Dryden, W. (ed.) (1984) *Individual Therapy in Britain*. London: Harper and Row.

Dryden, W. (1985) Challenging but not overwhelming: A compromise in negotiating homework assignments. *British Journal of Cognitive Therapy*, 3, 77–82.

Dryden, W. (1989a) Attributions, beliefs and constructs: Some points of comparison. In D. Lane (ed.), *Attributions, Beliefs and Constructs in Counselling Psychology*. Leicester: British Psychological Society.

Dryden, W. (ed.) (1989b) *Key Issues for Counselling in Action*. London: Sage.

Dryden, W. (1989c) The therapeutic alliance as an integrating framework. In W. Dryden (ed.), *Key Issues for Counselling in Action*. London: Sage.

Dryden, W. (1989d) The use of chaining in rational-emotive therapy. *Journal of Rational-Emotive Therapy*, 7, 59–66.

Dryden, W. (ed.) (1990) *Individual Therapy: A Handbook*. Milton Keynes: Open University Press.

Dryden, W. (1991) *Dryden on Counselling*, vol. 3. *Training and Supervision*. London: Whurr.

Dryden, W. (1992) *The Incredible Sulk*. London: Sheldon Press.

Duke, M.P. and Nowicki, S.J. (1982) A social learning analysis of interactional concepts and a multi-dimensional model of human interaction constellations. In J.C. Anakin and D.J. Kiesler (eds), *Handbook of Interpersonal Psychotherapy*. New York: Pergamon.

Egan, G. (1990) *The Skilled Helper: A Systematic Approach to Effective Helping*. California: Brooks/Cole.

Ellenberger, H.F. (1970) *The Discovery of the Unconscious. The History and Evolution of Dynamic Psychiatry*. New York: Basic Books.

Ellis, A. (1977a) Characteristics of psychotic and borderline psychotic individuals. In A. Ellis and R. Grieger (eds), *Handbook of Rational Emotive Therapy*. New York: Springer.

Ellis, A. (1977b) A rational approach to interpretation. In A. Ellis and R. Grieger (eds), *Handbook of Rational Emotive Therapy*. New York: Springer.

Ellis, A. and Whiteley, J.M. (eds) (1979) *Theoretical and Empirical Foundations of Rational Emotive Therapy*. California: Brooks/Cole.

Fennell, M.J.V. (1989) Depression. In K. Hawton, P.M. Salkovskis, J. Kirk and D.M. Clark (eds), *Cognitive Behaviour Therapy for Psychiatric Problems*. Oxford: Oxford University Press.

Ferguson, B. and Tyrer, P. (1989) Rating instruments in psychiatric research. In

C. Freeman and P. Tyrer (eds), *Research Methods in Psychiatry: A Beginner's Guide*. London: Gaskell/The Royal College of Psychiatrists.

Frank, E., Kupfer, D.J. and Perel, J.M. (1989) Early recurrence in unipolar depression. *Archives of General Psychiatry*, 46, 397–400.

Frank, J.D. (1982) Therapeutic components shared by psychotherapies. In J.H. Harvey and M.M. Parkes (eds), *Psychotherapy Research and Behavior Change*, vol. 1. Washington, DC: American Psychological Association.

Freeman, A., Simon, K.M., Beutler, L.E. and Arkowitz, H. (eds) (1989) *Comprehensive Handbook of Cognitive Therapy*. New York: Plenum.

Gilbert, P. (1984) *Depression: From Psychology to Brain State*. London: Lawrence Erlbaum Associates.

Gilbert, P. (1989) *Human Nature and Suffering*. London: Lawrence Erlbaum Associates.

Gilbert, P. (1992) *Depression: The Evolution of Powerlessness*. Hove: Lawrence Erlbaum, New York: Guilford Press.

Gilbert, P., Hughes, W. and Dryden, W. (1989) The therapist as the crucial variable in psychotherapy. In W. Dryden and L. Spurling (eds), *On Becoming a Psychotherapist*. London: Routledge.

Goldstein, A.P. and Michaels, G.Y. (1985) *Empathy: Development, Training and Consequences*. Hillsdale, NJ: Lawrence Erlbaum Associates.

Gotlib, I.H. and Cane, D.B. (1989) Self-report assessment of depression and anxiety. In P.C. Kendall and D. Watson (eds), *Anxiety and Depression: Distinctive and Overlapping Features*. New York: Academic Press.

Gotlib, I.H. and Colby, C.A. (1987) *Treatment of Depression: An Interpersonal Systems Approach*. New York: Pergamon Press.

Goudsmit, E.M. and Gadd, R. (1991) All in the mind? The psychologisation of illness. *The Psychologist: Bulletin of the British Psychological Society*, 4, 449–53.

Greenberg, L.S. (1979) Resolving splits: Use of the two-chair technique. *Psychotherapy, Theory, Research and Practice*, 16, 316–24.

Greenberg, L.S., Elliott, R.K. and Foerster, F.S (1990) Experiential processes in the psychotherapeutic treatment of depression. In C.D. McCann and N.S. Endler (eds), *Depression: New Directions in Theory, Research and Practice*. Toronto: Wall and Emerson.

Greenberg, L.S. and Safran, J.D. (1987) *Emotion in Psychotherapy*. New York: Guilford Press.

Grollman, E.A. (1988) *Suicide: Prevention, Intervention and Postvention*, 2nd edn. Boston: Beacon Press.

Guidano, V.F. and Liotti, G. (1983) *Cognitive Processes and Emotional Disorders*. New York: Guilford Press.

Gut, E. (1989) *Productive and Unproductive Depression: Success or Failure of a Vital Process*. London: Routledge and Kegan Paul.

Hawton, K. (1987) Assessment of suicide risk. *British Journal of Psychiatry*, 150, 145–53.

Hawton, K. and Catalan, J. (1987) *Attempted Suicide: A Practical Guide to its Nature and Management*. Oxford: Oxford University Press.

Heard, D.H. and Lake, B. (1986) The attachment dynamic in adult life. *British Journal of Psychiatry*, 149, 430–8.

Hollon, S.D. and Kriss, M.R. (1984) Cognitive factors in clinical research and practice. *Clinical Psychology Review*, 4, 35–76.

Hollon, S.D., Shelton, R.C. and Loosen, P.T. (1991) Cognitive therapy and pharmacotherapy for depression. *Journal of Consulting and Clinical Psychology*, 59, 88–99.

Hooley, T.M. and Teasdale, J.D. (1989) Predictors of relapse in unipolar depressives: Expressed emotion, marital distress and perceived criticism. *Journal of Abnormal Psychology*, 98, 229–35.

Horowitz, L.M. and Vitkus, J. (1986) The interpersonal basis of psychiatric symptoms. *Clinical Psychology Review*, 6, 443–70.

Jack, R.L. and Williams, J.M.G. (1991) Attribution and intervention in self-poisoning. *British Journal of Medical Psychology*, 64, 345–58.

Janoff-Bulman, R. (1979) Characterological versus behavioral self-blame: Inquiries into depression and rape. *Journal of Personality and Social Psychology*, 37, 1798–809.

Janoff-Bulman, R. and Hecker, B. (1988) Depression, vulnerability, and world assumptions. In L.B. Alloy (ed.), *Cognitive Processes in Depression*. New York: Guilford Press.

Jehu, D. (1988) *Beyond Childhood Abuse: Therapy for Women who were Childhood Victims*. Chichester: Wiley.

Jehu, D. (1989) Mood disturbances among women clients abused in childhood: Prevalence, etiology and treatment. *Journal of Interpersonal Violence*, 4, 164–84.

Kahn, E. (1985) Heinz Kohut and Carl Rogers: A timely comparison. *American Psychologist*, 40, 893–904.

Kahn, E. (1989) Heinz Kohut and Carl Rogers: Towards a constructive collaboration. *Psychotherapy*, 26, 555–63.

Karasu, T.B. (1990) Toward a clinical model of the psychotherapy for depression, II: An integrative and selective treatment approach. *American Journal of Psychiatry*, 147, 269–78.

Kasper, S. and Rosenthal, N.E. (1989) Anxiety and depression in seasonal affective disorder. In P.C. Kendall and D. Watson (eds), *Anxiety and Depression: Distinctive and Overlapping Features*. New York: Academic Press.

Katakis, C.D. (1989) Stages of psychotherapy: Progressive reconceptualisation as a self-organizing process. *Psychotherapy*, 26, 484–93.

Kegan, R. (1982) *The Evolving Self: Problem and Process in Human Development*. Cambridge, MA: Harvard University Press.

Kelly, G. (1955) *The Psychology of Personal Constructs*. New York: Norton and Co.

Klass, E.T. (1990) Guilt, shame, and embarrassment: Cognitive-behavioural approaches. In H. Leitenberg (ed.), *Handbook of Social and Evaluation Anxiety*. New York: Plenum.

Klerman, G.L. (1988) The current age of youthful melancholia: Evidence for increase in depression among adolescents and young adults. *British Journal of Psychiatry*, 152, 4–14.

Klerman, G.L., Weissman, M.M., Rounsaville, B.J. and Chevon, E.S. (1984) *Interpersonal Psychotherapy of Depression*. New York: Basic Books.

Kohut, H. (1977) *The Restoration of the Self*. New York: International Universities Press.

Kuiper, N.A. (1988) Vulnerability and episodic cognitions in a self-worth contingency model of depression. In L.B. Alloy (ed.), *Cognitive Processes in Depression*. New York: Guilford Press.

Kuiper, N.A. and Olinger, L.J. (1986) Dysfunctional attitudes and a self-worth contingency model of depression. In P.C. Kendall (ed.), *Advances in Cognitive-*

*Behavioral Research and Therapy*. New York: Academic Press.

Leary, T. (1957) *The Interpersonal Diagnosis of Personality*. New York: Ronald Press.

Lewis, H.B. (1986) The role of shame in depression. In M. Rutter, C.E. Izard and P.B. Read (eds), *Depression in Young People: Developmental and Clinical Perspectives*. New York: Guilford Press.

Lewis, H.B. (1987a) Introduction: Shame – the 'sleeper' in psychopathology. In H.B. Lewis (ed.), *The Role of Shame in Symptom Formation*. Hillsdale, NJ: Lawrence Erlbaum Associates.

Lewis, H.B. (ed.) (1987b) *The Role of Shame in Symptom Formation*. Hillsdale, NJ: Lawrence Erlbaum Associates.

Liotti, G. (1988) Attachment and cognition: A guide for the reconstruction of early pathogenic experiences in cognitive therapy. In C. Perris, I.M. Blackburn and H. Perris (eds), *Handbook of Cognitive Psychotherapy*. New York: Springer.

Mahoney, M.J. and Gabriel, T.J. (1987) Psychotherapy and cognitive science. *Journal of Cognitive Psychotherapy: An International Quarterly*, 1, 39–60.

Margulies, A. (1984) Toward empathy: The uses of wonder. *American Journal of Psychiatry*, 141, 1025–33.

McCann, I.L., Sakheim, D.K. and Abrahamson, D.J (1988) Trauma and victimization: A model of psychological adaptation. *The Counselling Psychologist*, 16, 531–94.

Miller, I.J. (1989) The therapeutic empathic communication (TEC) process. *American Journal of Psychotherapy*, 43, 531–45.

Mollon, P. (1984) Shame in relation to narcissistic disturbance. *British Journal of Medical Psychology*, 57, 207–14.

Mollon, P. and Parry, G. (1984) The fragile self: Narcissistic disturbance and the protective function of depression. *British Journal of Medical Psychology*, 57, 137–45.

Moretti, M.M., Higgins, E.T. and Feldman, L.A. (1990) The self-system in depression: Conceptualization and treatment. In C.D. McCann and N.S. Endler (eds), *Depression: New Directions in Theory, Research and Practice*. Toronto: Wall and Emerson.

Morrison, A.P. (1984) Shame and the psychology of the self. In P.E. Stepansky and A. Goldberg (eds), *Kohut's Legacy: Contributions to Self Psychology*. New York: Analytic Press/Lawrence Erlbaum Associates.

Murphy, H.B.M. (1978) The advent of guilt feelings as a common depressive symptom: A historical comparison on two continents. *Psychiatry*, 41, 229–42.

Nathanson, D.L. (ed.) (1987) *The Many Faces of Shame*. New York: Guilford Press.

Nesse, R.M. (1990) Evolutionary explanations of emotions. *Human Nature*, 1, 261–89.

Oatley, K. and Boulton, W. (1985) A social theory of depression in reaction to life events. *Psychological Review*, 92, 372–88.

Paykel, E. (1989) The background: Extent and nature of the disorder. In K. Herbst and E. Paykel (eds), *Depression: An Integrative Approach*. Oxford: Heinemann Medical Books.

Pennebaker, J.W. (1988) Confiding traumatic experiences and health. In S. Fisher and J. Reason (eds), *Handbook of Life Stress, Cognition and Health*. Chichester: Wiley.

Pennebaker, J.W. and Becall, S.K. (1986) Confronting a traumatic event: Toward an understanding of inhibition and disease. *Journal of Abnormal Psychology*, 95, 274–87.

Peselow, E.D., Robins, C.J., Block, P., Barouche, F.M. and Fieve, R.R. (1990) Dysfunctional attitudes in depressed patients before and after clinical treatment and normal control subjects. *American Journal of Psychiatry*, 147, 439–44.

Pyszczynski, T. and Greenberg, J. (1987) Self-regulatory perseveration and the depressive self-focusing style: A self-awareness theory of reactive depression. *Psychological Bulletin*, 102, 122–38.

Rogers, C. (1957) The necessary and sufficient conditions of therapeutic change. *Journal of Consulting Psychology*, 21, 95–103.

Rosen, H. (1989) Piagetian theory and cognitive therapy. In C. Freeman and P. Tyrer (eds), *Research Methods in Psychiatry: A Beginner's Guide*. London: Gaskell/The Royal College of Psychiatrists.

Ryle, A. (1990) *Cognitive-Analytic Therapy: Active Participation in Change*. Chichester: Wiley.

Safran, J.D. and Segal, Z.V. (1990) *Interpersonal Process in Cognitive Therapy*. New York: Basic Books.

Schore, A.N. (1991) Early superego development: The emergence of shame and narcissistic affect regulation in the practicing period. *Psychoanalysis and Contemporary Thought. A Quarterly of Integrative and Interdisciplinary Studies*, 14, 187–250.

Scott, J. (1988) Chronic depression. *British Journal of Psychiatry*, 153, 287–97.

Seligman, M.E.P. (1975) *Helplessness: On Depression Development and Death*. San Francisco: Freeman and Co.

Seligman, M.E.P. (1989) Explanatory style: Predicting depression, achievement and health. In M.D. Yapko (ed.), *Brief Approaches to Treating Anxiety and Depression*. New York: Brunner/Mazel.

Sholomskas, D.E. (1990) Interviewing methods. In B.B. Wolman and G. Stricker (eds), *Depressive Disorders: Facts, Theories and Treatment Methods*. New York: Wiley.

Skouholt, T.M. and Rønnestad, M.H. (1992) The Evolving Professional Self: Stages and Themes in Therapist and Counselor Development. Chichester: Wiley.

Swallow, S.R. and Kuiper, N.A. (1988) Social comparison and negative self evaluation: An application to depression. *Clinical Psychology Review*, 8, 55–76.

Taylor, S.E. and Brown, J.D. (1988) Illusion and well being: A social psychological perspective on mental health. *Psychological Bulletin*, 103, 193–210.

Teasdale, J.D. and Dent, J. (1987) Cognitive vulnerability to depression: An investigation of two hypotheses. *British Journal of Clinical Psychology*, 26, 113–26.

Trower, P., Casey, A. and Dryden, W. (1988) *Cognitive-behavioural Counselling in Action*. London: Sage.

Vasile, R.G., Samson, J.A., Bemporad, J., Bloomingdale, K.L., Creasey, D., Fenton, B.T., Gudeman, J.E. and Schildkraut, J.J. (1987) A biopsychosocial approach to treating patients with affective disorders. *American Journal of Psychiatry*, 144, 341–4.

Ward, D.E. (1989) Termination of individual counselling: Concepts. In W. Dryden (ed.), *Key Issues for Counselling in Action*. London: Sage.

Watkins, C.E. (1989a) Transference phenomena in the counselling situation. In W. Dryden (ed.), *Key Issues for Counselling in Action*. London: Sage.

Watkins, C.E. (1989b) Countertransference: Its impact on the counselling situation. In W. Dryden (ed.), *Key Issues for Counselling in Action*. London: Sage.

Williams, J.M.G. and Wells, J. (1989) Suicide patients. In J. Scott, J.M.G. Williams and A.T. Beck (eds), *Cognitive Therapy in Clinical Practice: An Illustrative Casebook. Practice*. London: Routledge.

Wolf, E.S. (1988) *Treating the Self: Elements of Clinical Self Psychology*. New York: Guilford Press.

Yalom, I.D. (1980) *Existential Psychotherapy*. New York: Basic Books.

# Index